Advanced English

Contents

BOOK MAP

	Unit 1	Unit 2	Unit 3	Unit 4
Focus	**Advertising** **Advertisements:** rights, wrongs and methods	**The environment** **Environmental issues:** global warming, pollution and man	**What's in the news?** **Current affairs:** news, reporting and the media	**Medical matters** **Health:** keeping fit, illnesses and disease
Functions	Talking about opinions Expressing preferences Criticising Questioning	Hypothesising Giving reasons Explaining Describing graphs and statistics	Debating Expressing ideas Correcting Agreeing / disagreeing	Describing symptoms Giving opinions
Skills	**Reading:** Advertising guidelines, opinions about advertising, a report about a survey about advertising in the UK **Writing:** An advertisement for an unusual product, writing about classmates' opinions, a product review **Listening:** A radio interview about advertising in schools, radio advertisements **Speaking:** A debate, interviewing someone, planning an article	**Reading:** A text about global warming, and article about endangered species, a description of the greenhouse effect **Writing:** A leaflet about environmental issues, describing graphs and statistics **Listening:** A lecture on pollution, note taking, a radio programme about recycling and re-using **Speaking:** Discussing environmental issues, endangered species, pollution, describing pictures, talking hypothetically	**Reading:** *Killer Wave Drowns Asia, Blog or die!*, a blog entry, a guide to satellite TV **Writing:** Newspaper genre, writing newspaper headlines, paragraph writing **Listening:** A news report about a media mogul, an interview about media ownership, a radio programme about censorship, preposition errors **Speaking:** Discussing how the media portrays events	**Reading:** *AIDS Awareness, Healthcare around the world: the NHS* **Writing:** Writing an article, correcting your own mistakes **Listening:** A lecture on heart disease, a dictation **Speaking:** Improving hospital performance, allergies and illnesses, describing symptoms, comparing health-care systems
Grammar	Dependent prepositions Co-ordinating and subordinating conjunctions Modal auxiliaries	Conditional review Conditional advanced points	Prepositions	Adverbial clauses Conjunctions Common errors
Vocabulary / Pronunciation	The language of advertising, collocations, synonyms	The environment, scientific words, actions, everyday objects	The language of the media, working words and expressions out from the context, synonyms, compound nouns, newspaper headline words	Medical terminology, diseases and illnesses, doctors and health-care professionals, medical idioms

Unit 5	Unit 6	Unit 7	Unit 8	
Risky business!	**The best days of your life**	**Language and life**	**Words, words, words**	Focus
Risk taking: life, death and personal	**Education:** schools, colleges and universities	**Language:** learning, using and living	**Words:** written, spoken and developments	
Encouraging Discouraging Comparing Recounting	Comparing Contrasting Debating Arguing a point	Correcting Describing Assessing Defining Analysing Advising	Describing language Ordering Giving opinions Identifying speakers Planning Collaborating	Functions
Reading: *Out on her own*: an article about taking risks in your job, quotations about risks, *The world's greatest gambler* **Writing:** An email giving advice, writing a pamphlet **Listening:** A lecture about risk taking behaviour, a conversation about bungee-jumping **Speaking:** Risks you have taken, reacting to quotations, encouragement and advice	**Reading:** The English education system, child prodigies, *Education for the masses* **Writing:** Essay about education, writing a personal statement **Listening:** Radio interview about truancy, an interview about home schooling and prodigies **Speaking:** Discussing school days, debate about home schooling	**Reading:** *Double the fun?*: an article on bilingualism, a letter of advice **Writing:** Essay on why you are studying English, writing a letter **Listening:** Vox pops about language and learning, conversation discussing a lecture, advice about dyslexia **Speaking:** Assessing your language skills, language in general	**Reading:** Notes, *From Varro to Gates*: encyclopaedias through the ages **Writing:** Short paragraphs, a research-based project, a biography **Listening:** A lecture about dictionaries, a tutorial session about sources **Speaking:** Discussing words in English, talking about reference media, planning a project	Skills
Conjunctions	Punctuation	Prefixes Suffixes	Verb forms Prepositions	Grammar
Collocations, set phrases about risk taking, dangerous sports, animal idioms, word building	Words connected with education, dependent prepositions, phrases with 'play', words about punishments, punctuation mark names, school / college subjects	Prefixes, suffixes, words connected with language, synonyms	Words about words, types of reference book, defining words, words in context, expressions with 'by', word building	Vocabulary / Pronunciation

Advanced English **2**
(CEF version) C1

Signum International
S.a.r.l. Luxembourg, Zug Branch
Zeughausgasse 9a
6301 Zug
Switzerland

© Signum International
S.à.r.l. Luxembourg,
Zug Branch, Zug, 2009

First published 2009
This impression (lowest digit)
    7 9 10 8 6
ISBN 978-3-03758-078-3

Acknowledgements
EF Education First would like to thank the many teachers, academic directors, and language experts who have participated in the development of EF's library of educational materials. Beata Schmid, Ph.D. and the faculty members of EF schools worldwide have contributed to the continual development, implementation, assessment and revision of this series. The following EF International Language Schools (ILS) faculty members and writers created material for the 3rd Edition of EF's Efekta™ System General English textbook series.

Cheryl Albright (ILS Seattle)
Ludmila Andersson (ILS Brisbane)
Laurie Barlow (ILS Vancouver)
Rena Bartlett (ILS Boston)
Sophie Behagg (ILS Brighton)
Jason Berry (ILS Boston)
Jamie Collinson (ILS London)
Ian Devey (ILS Bournemouth)
Kirsty Dickson (ILS Vancouver)
Sandy Dzogan (ILS Toronto)
Thomas Engfer (ILS Los Angeles)
Sarah Finck (ILS Boston)
Damian Flores (ILS Miami)
Monica Guerrero (ILS Miami)

Lisa Guglielmi (ILS Vancouver)
Neil Hammond (ILS Vancouver)
Grant Hitchcock (ILS Brighton)
Ted Kelsey (ILS New York)
Leslie Lloyd (ILS Santa Barbara)
Luca Marchiori (ILS Bournemouth)
Kristy McKee (ILS Santa Barbara)
Corinne Meers (ILS Sydney)
Hans Mol (SCC Australia)
Kim Nowitsky (ILS Vancouver)
Samantha Palfrey (ILS Toronto)
Vaughan Thomas
Carol Uy (ILS Toronto)
Elise Guillen (ILS Vancouver)

Design:	Masterpress (Hong Kong) Ltd.
Printing:	Hon Cheong Printing Ltd.
Photography:	Getty Images
Audio Production:	Southern Cross Connexxions / Fracas, Australia
Development Editors:	Jane Lee, Luca Marchiori, Celia Wigley
Level Editors:	Kirsten Campbell-Howes, Aelred Doyle, Erika Fässler-Nelson, Luca Marchiori, Hans Mol
Publisher:	Jane Lee
Editorial Director:	Christopher McCormick, Ph.D.

Printed in Hong Kong

EF Education First is committed to producing materials using environmentally friendly papers, materials and processes. The selected papers meet rigorous standards for forest management as well as production. This title has been printed with the following paper: UPM Paper.

Advertising

After this unit, you should be able to ...

- Listen to a radio programme
- Use conjunctions
- Use advertising vocabulary
- Interview people
- Read and interpret survey results
- Write a product review

A You find advertisements in a large variety of places. With a partner draw up a list and compare this with others. Which of these places do you consider to be more successful than others, and why? Are there any media forms which you dislike? Why?

B Look at the advertisements your teacher gives you. Explain why you think one advertisement is more successful than another.

C Can you recall any of your favourite advertisements? Perhaps you can even download some from the Internet. Why do / did you like them so much?

Listening and Speaking

A Are there any places which are particularly inappropriate for advertisements? Does this depend on the product being advertised?

B Listen to a radio programme. Who are the speakers and what is being discussed?

Speaker 1 _____

Speaker 2 _____

Speaker 3 _____

Topic _____

D Read your notes from Exercise C again. Add at least four more points of your own. Which ideas do you agree / disagree with? Why?

_____

_____

_____

_____

_____

C Can you remember the opinions of the two speakers? Complete the table. Listen again to check your answers.

Speaker 2 For / against?

_____
_____
_____

Main points

_____
_____
_____
_____
_____
_____
_____

Speaker 3 For / against?

_____
_____
_____

Main points

_____
_____
_____
_____
_____
_____
_____
_____
_____

E Study the vocabulary from the audio below. Which words do you think each word is followed by? Listen again to check your answers.

1 bombarded _____

2 cooperate

3 in return *водмен, вовет*

4 familiar *знакомый, близкий хорошо знать*

5 the role that advertising _____

6 sponsored _____

7 commission ✓

8 example

9 appeal *обращение, образование,*

10 hard to come *трудно найти*

11 exposed *открытый, объявлен.*

12 unique

13 (to be) up *быть в курсе*

14 think very carefully *думай хорошенько*

15 agree *согласна*

16 contributing *способствуй, ассистуя*

F Here are some phrases we can use to express our opinions and preferences.
Can you put them in the correct column?

③ Don't you think it would be better ...?   I don't agree. ①   But what about ...? ①
① I'm afraid I don't agree.   I don't think that ... ①   Frankly, I doubt if ... ①
③ The truth of the matter is ...   I'd rather ... ①   The way I see it ... 1-2
② As far as I'm concerned ... *насколько я могу судить*   If it were up to me ... ?   I suspect that ... ①
② I think ...   I'm pretty sure that ... ②   I'm convinced that ... 2
② Without a doubt ...   The reason why ... ③   When you consider that ... 2-3
③ For this reason ... *по этой причине*   Considering ... *учитывая, принимая во внимание*   That's why ... ③

disagreeing ①	opinions, preferences ②	giving reasons and offering explanations

G Work in two groups. One group is for advertising in schools and the other is against it. Prepare your opening argument with your group. It should be about five minutes long and contain your main ideas.

Take turns presenting your opening argument. Listen to the other group and take notes for rebuttal, as they speak. Proceed like this until you have run out of ideas and / or rebuttal and a conclusion is reached.

H Use the vocabulary from Exercise C to complete the gaps.

1 This style of cooking is _unique_ to our region.
2 If it were _appealing_ to me, I wouldn't allow him back in the house.
3 I'm not that _familiar_ with this computer programme.
4 The movie _____ him to some pretty foul language.
5 I mowed her lawn _____ for a home-made cake.
6 My boss _is up_ three thousand dollars to my raise.

Homework

Think back on the debate. Has your initial point of view changed now? Why / why not? Discuss this in a 200-word essay and bring this to class next time.

Grammar and Writing

A Read the following lines from the radio programme from the previous section. Fill in the correct conjunction and describe the connection between the ideas. Then read through the audio script to check you have chosen the correct conjunction.

> **■ EXAMPLE**
>
> *It is true that certain fast food companies advertise in schools <u>but</u> these advertisements tend to be quite subtle ...*
>
> *connection: contrast*

1 At home, they can turn the TV off, _____ their parents can and advertising can be avoided.

2 We are all familiar with the role that advertising and sponsorship play in sport _____ ...

3 We are constantly bombarded by images on billboards and posters _____ outside ...

4 I think it sounds like an experiment which could benefit schools greatly _____ carried out responsibly.

5 ... but recently it has been suggested that advertising should be allowed in an area which has _____ now been sacrosanct ...

6 ... it is something we have been seeing increasingly _____ the late 1990s.

7 Many schools are finding it hard to maintain their buildings as well as buying educational materials, _____ this is something that local authorities are becoming interested in.

B Most conjunctions are co-ordinating or subordinating. Can you divide the conjunctions from Exercise A into these two categories and can you add any more examples to them?

co-ordinating conjunctions

subordinating conjunctions

C Choose an advertisement from a newspaper or magazine which appeals to you and a classmate. Write down its positive points. Are there are any ways you think it could be improved and made more effective? Compare your advertisement with another pair. Did you choose similar kinds of advertisements? Did you like your advertisement for similar reasons?

D Underline all the conjunctions in your advertisement and discuss which kind they are and why they are being used.

E 'Chindogu' are highly unusual Japanese inventions designed to make life that little bit easier. Often they seem extremely unmarketable and useless. Choose one product from the list to advertise with your partner from the list below.

1   Umbrella tube   2   Daddy nurser

3   Butter stick   4   Double-bristled toothbrush

5   Solar-powered cigarette lighter

6   Baby mop

F With your partner compose a list of all the possible positive points of the invention you have chosen. You need to make your product appear worthwhile to the consumer.

> ▇ EXAMPLE
> *The butter stick is a convenient size so you can take it with you wherever you go.*

1   _____

2   _____
    _____

3   _____
    _____

4   _____

5   _____

6   _____

G Write a three paragraph advertisement for your invention using the conjunctions from Exercise C and your notes from Exercises E and F.

H Make a copy of your advertisement but without the conjunctions. Give it to another pair and see if they can fill in the correct conjunctions.

I Take turns presenting your chosen invention to the rest of the class. Listen to the other groups and take a note of the positive points of each in the table below. In small groups discuss which invention is the most unusual / the funniest etc.

invention	positive points

Listening and Speaking

A Should advertising be regulated? Why? Why not? Who regulates advertising in your country?

_____
_____
_____
_____
_____
_____
_____
_____
_____
_____

B Read the following guidelines for good advertising. Match a topic on the left to an explanation on the right.

1 Substantiation

2 Social responsibility

3 Infomercials

4 Alcohol

5 Cars

6 Medical claims

7 Illnesses

8 Slimming

9 Shampoo

a Claims should never be made concerning serious diseases such as cancer, HIV or heart disease.

b Claims that it can lead to healthier or thicker hair must be substantiated.

c It should be obvious that it is an advertisement and not a documentary.

d Precise amounts of weight loss may not be mentioned.

e All claims made for the product should be able to be proved.

f Speed and acceleration should never be the main advertising features.

g The advertisement should not encourage illegal or irresponsible behaviour.

h This should never be marketed at anybody under the age of 18. Anybody seen drinking should appear over the age of 30.

i These can only be made for legally licensed medicines.

C Listen to four radio advertisements. What are they advertising?

1 _____
2 _____
3 _____
4 _____

D Answer the following questions from memory. Listen once more to check.

1 How does Ultraslim describe their potential customers' weight? _____

2 What can Ultraslim help you to avoid?
_____

3 What is special about the Dacona 500 GTI's interior and entertainment system? _____

4 Extra space has been devoted to which area of the car? _____

5 What does Dazzle shampoo stimulate? _____

6 Using Dazzle shampoo is an alternative to doing what on a bad-hair day? _____

7 How does Cranberry Crush taste? _____

8 What kind of feeling do you get from drinking it? _____

E Which of the guidelines in Exercise B apply to which advert? Complete the second column of the table.

Guideline number	Reasons
Advertisement 1	
Advertisement 2	
Advertisement 3	
Advertisement 4	

F Listen again. Do the adverts answer to the guidelines? Give reasons as to why they do or don't.

G Rewrite the advertisements so that they answer to the guidelines. Then perform the adverts in groups as if it was being played for radio or television.

H Interview your classmates using the following questions. Take notes of their answers.

question	name and answer
1 Do you think advertising really influences you to buy things? If so, what?	
2 Does being manipulated by advertisements bother you? Give reasons.	
3 Do you think advertising is an art form?	
4 What do you think of subliminal advertising (ads which work on peoples' unconscious minds)?	
5 How does advertising in your country vary from advertising in other countries?	
6 Which medium do you think is most effective for advertising? Why?	
7 Would you ever buy a product solely because of an advertisement?	
8 Are there any products in your country which are not allowed to be advertised?	

I Choose a classmate whose opinions you found most interesting. Write three paragraphs to convey their opinions. Begin by writing how they feel generally about advertising and then move on to give more specific information and personal examples. Use a variety of conjunctions in your writing.

EXAMPLE

Kenji is generally quite supportive of most forms of advertising if it is ethical.

He especially enjoys advertisements that employ humour, such as ...

Vocabulary

Read the quotations about advertising. For every quotation decide how old you think each person is, what sex they are and what kind of person they are.

1 I think the media has a huge influence on us, in determining the kinds of products we buy, and I'm not ashamed to admit that I'm manipulated by advertising. If I see an advertisement for a new brand of toothpaste, for example, and I'm not happy with my current one, well, I'll give it a go and why not? There are so many different products out there now. It's so exciting in comparison to twenty years ago when there weren't as many. I love going to my local supermarket and picking up something new. Advertising is a way of helping you to try something new, and what's so bad about that?

age _____   sex _____   personality _____

2 I recently went along to one of those nights where they get you to try new products and then people ask you questions about them. This one was for new chocolate bars, it was great. We got to try two different kinds and then rank them according to taste, texture etc. One of them is one of the most popular chocolate bars at the moment and we had to compare the new one to it. We didn't get paid but we got a lot of free chocolate bars to take home with us.

age _____   sex _____   personality _____

3 I try to ignore advertising as much as possible, but it is becoming increasingly difficult these days. I don't own a television or a computer so I'm not constantly bombarded by ads but I do see them in the newspaper and the occasional magazine. I use the same brands now as I did ten years ago. I don't believe all those fancy promises they make to you anyway. Shoe polish is shoe polish; it can't make you a cup of tea now, can it?

age _____   sex _____   personality _____

4 We are going to unleash this new and improved product next month. Soon everyone in this country will be buying it. You'll be able to buy it at supermarkets, service stations, convenience stores ... We asked the public how they felt about the old version about a year ago and the results were a little disappointing so we knew we could do better. It will be advertised in magazines, on TV, on billboards ... I'm sure it's going to be a huge success.

age _____   sex _____   personality _____

B Match a word on the left to a collocation on the right. Discuss with a partner what these collocations mean. Which collocations refer to which extracts?

1	brand	☐		☐	a	communication
2	opinion	☐		☐	b	of purchase
3	market	☐		☐	c	strategy
4	point	☐		☐	d	poll
5	mass	☐		☐	e	loyalty
6	advertising	☐		☐	f	release
7	media	☐		☐	g	leader
8	press	☐		☐	h	campaign

C Read the extracts again and find the synonyms for the following words.

1 deciding _____

2 influence unfairly _____

3 present _____

4 try _____

5 classify _____

6 in keeping to _____

7 attacked _____

8 extravagant _____

9 set free _____

10 not good _____

D Test a classmate. Define one of the words from the extracts and see if they can guess it.

E Which of extracts from Exercise A is closest to your own attitude to advertising? Phrase five questions to ask fellow classmates to find out if their opinions are at all similar to any of the extracts. Interview three classmates and ask them your questions. Take a note of their answers.

> **■ EXAMPLE**
> *Have you ever or would you ever participate in market research?*

1 _____
_____

2 _____
_____

3 _____

4 _____
_____

5 _____
_____

F Complete each gap with an appropriate conjunction.

The most traditional form of advertising is in newspapers (1) _____ magazines. It can be extremely expensive, especially (2) _____ the publication has national circulation. (3) _____, putting the right advertisement in the right publication can be a good investment. A good starting point for consideration is who you want to see the advert. That will help you to choose the right publication. (4) _____ you may want a national profile, (5) _____ the majority of your customers are local, then advertise locally. Also, look to see who else advertises in the magazine. (6) _____ they are all in a similar line of business, it is obviously a good place to start.

Homework

Interview a native speaker about their attitudes to advertising in their country. Write down ten questions to ask first, using the vocabulary you have learnt in this lesson. Take extensive notes during the interview. Bring these to the next class to compare results with your fellow classmates.

Reading

A What role do you think advertising plays in society today? Would you consider this a good role or a bad one? How would you describe the role it plays in terms of business and human behaviour.

B Study the article. The first sentence of each paragraph has been removed. Put them back in the right place.

1 The survey, carried out nationwide, asked a wide range of people about what they felt the role of advertising was in this country. The resulting picture which has emerged could help both advertisers and regulators alike.

2 One of the most interesting effects of this is that there is a large amount of nostalgia attached to advertisements from days gone by, particularly ones which were around during people's childhood.

3 Respondents to the survey often spoke of the process of 'advert hopping' where they would flick from TV channel to TV channel watching the adverts rather than the programmes they accompanied. People also mentioned fondly series of adverts which tell a story or feature the same characters.

4 People are aware of the costs involved in television advertising and assumed that the more advertising you could afford the better your business was doing. A few respondents expressed the opposite view, citing a large high street retailer who famously never advertises on television.

5 This ranges therefore from the packaging a product comes in, to full-blown television adverts.

6 Many people said that advertising was useful and saved you time when going shopping as you knew what products were available. If there was no advertising, a lot of time would be wasted walking round shops looking to see what there was to buy.

7 Without the sponsorship that advertising provides, many sporting events would be prohibitively expensive and might not take place. On a related point, people were aware that as all the TV licence fee goes to the BBC, without advertising, there would be no other channels on TV.

8 Although many respondents said they often found advertising annoying and intrusive, they agreed on the whole that it was a central and valuable part of daily life and losing it would leave a gap in our culture.

a As part of the day-to-day culture of the UK, advertising is seen as a form of entertainment for many of us.

b Such an overwhelmingly positive view of the role of adverts in today's society may be very encouraging for those who want us to buy their products.

c A recent survey by a leading advertising agency has built up a very interesting picture of how the British public view advertising.

d A view that was particularly prevalent was that advertising was beneficial to society in the way that it funds sporting events.

e One of the most interesting conclusions was that people view advertising as a part of contemporary culture, in the same way that they view music, film, television and the print media.

f Most respondents to the survey felt that if a brand is constantly being advertised, it was an indication that it was doing well.

g A further benefit that people felt advertising engendered was the dissemination of information.

h When asked what constituted advertising, the prevailing view was that it is anything that contains a company name or logo.

1		5	
2		6	
3		7	
4		8	

C Read the text in Exercise B again. Find words that mean the following:

1 throughout the whole country (Paragraph 1)

_____

2 to move from one to the other very quickly (Paragraph 3) _____

3 someone who sells something (Paragraph 4)

_____

4 completely developed (Paragraph 5)

_____

5 discouragingly (Paragraph 7)

_____

6 people who reply (Paragraph 8)

_____

D Find two examples, in the text, of new vocabulary for each part of speech listed below.

verb	noun	adjective	adverb

E You are going to construct a questionnaire to learn more about people's views on advertising. With a fellow student, talk about what you would like to find out, such as how people feel about ad breaks during TV programmes. Write down eight 'things to find out' below.

F Turn you ideas into questions to ask. Try to use a variety of different questions such as open-ended questions, multiple choice questions etc.

G Interview four different people outside class, two men and two women. Ask people who vary in age, profession etc, in order to get more accurate findings. Take extensive notes during the interview.

H Study the article in Exercise B again. Go through it and underline any vocabulary you can use to write a similar article.

I Plan your article. It should include at least four paragraphs. The first paragraph should introduce what you are attempting to do, and the last should draw conclusions about what you found out. The body of your article must contain the main ideas. Share your plan with a classmate. Write the first draft of your article and let a fellow student read it for peer review.

Writing

A Study the products in the photos. Do you own all of them? If so, what brands or makes of these products do you own? Are you happy with their performance or would you like to try another brand or make? How could they be improved? If you don't own any of these products, which brands or makes would you consider buying?

B Match the product reviews to the products in Exercise A.

1 _____ Sporty yet sophisticated. It has plenty of new additions which make it that much more enjoyable. It handles like a dream and its entertainment system is to die for.

2 _____ A bold new look sets these apart from the pack. Certainly not for those who like to blend into the crowd. Extremely comfortable, it's like you're walking on thin air!

3 _____ Totally over-priced and a real let down. The buttons are far too small and the graphics are lame.

4 _____ It is the slimmest one I've ever seen, your friends will be green with envy when they see you with this little number. It has a huge memory and produces consistently good shots.

5 _____ Extremely practical but a little disappointing in the looks department. Water-resistant to 200 metres with an in-built stopwatch.

6 _____ Another winner from one of our most beloved brands, though they're not for everyone. They are moderately priced and their casual street style will especially appeal to those under 25.

7 _____ Several new features are included in the key board. It comes with Windows XP ® Home Edition and offers a free upgrade to 160 GB.

C Look at the products in Exercise B again. Write down sentences to show how you feel about them using modal auxiliaries such as 'have to', 'need to', 'must', 'should', etc.

EXAMPLE

I have to buy new sneakers at least once a month. Otherwise, I feel like I'm out of step with the latest fashions.

1 _____

_____

2 _____

_____

3 _____

_____

4 _____

_____

D Underline the new words and / or phrases in the reviews in Exercise B. Check their meaning with a partner and / or a dictionary.

E What do consumers need to consider before buying any product or service? Draw up a list with a classmate and explain. Does the type of product or service make you look at different things?

what to consider	reason	type of product or service
price	Consumers need to consider price because ...	electronics

F Study your list from Exercise E. How important are each of these to you? Rank them and compare with a partner. How would you explain differences between people?

G In pairs choose four brands or makes of a particular product or service and make notes about the pros and cons of each in terms of size and so on using the list in Exercise E. Compare your notes with another pair.

H Choose two products from Exercise G to write 50-75 word reviews on. Use the new vocabulary you have learned.

I Read three classmates reviews. Tick the box if you feel they fulfil the criteria.

1 1 ☐   2 ☐   3 ☐
Is the review clear and well-structured?

2 1 ☐   2 ☐   3 ☐
Does it grab the reader's attention and make them want to know more about the product?

3 1 ☐   2 ☐   3 ☐
Is it informative, using specific examples?

4 1 ☐   2 ☐   3 ☐
Does it convey a strong opinion?

5 1 ☐   2 ☐   3 ☐
Does it use new vocabulary learned in this lesson and the rest of the unit?

6 1 ☐   2 ☐   3 ☐
Are all words spelt correctly?

7 1 ☐   2 ☐   3 ☐
Is it long enough?

8 1 ☐   2 ☐   3 ☐
Does it use a variety of grammatical structures correctly?

9 1 ☐   2 ☐   3 ☐
Is its style appropriate to a review?

10 1 ☐   2 ☐   3 ☐
Is the handwriting easy to read?

J Now share your reviews again in small groups and take into account their answers to the questions concerning your review. Ask other students to refer specifically to parts of your review that they feel need improvement.

Language Practice

A Fill the gaps with appropriate conjunctions.

1 Adverts are always more successful _____ they have a famous actor in them.

2 Sales of toys increase dramatically after advertisements _____ children employ 'pester-power'.

3 Surveys suggest that women feel better _____ watching adverts for chocolate.

4 Billboard adverts are successful _____ TV advertising is often more effective.

5 In many countries, advertising smoking is banned _____ governments are worried about people's health.

6 Alcohol advertising is a contentious issue _____ many people feel very strongly about.

7 Advertising is a multi-million dollar business _____ it is quite cut-throat.

8 People often see an advert once or twice _____ realising what it is advertising.

9 Most companies advertise on television _____ on the radio—rarely both.

10 Let me know _____ you have seen the new advert.

B How could you edit these sentences to be clearer with fewer words?

1 Nowadays people are more sophisticated and so they react to adverts differently from how they did thirty years ago.

2 People do not trust companies if it is apparent that they are indulging in the 'hard-sell'.

3 Television advertising is regulated by governments or it is regulated by the television companies themselves.

4 Adverts are often repeated until they are no longer considered to be bringing in new sales.

5 People often feel that advertising at children is immoral but people are often happy to see advertisements aimed at teenagers.

6 Advertising campaigns often become very popular once they are aired.

C Join the sentences together with appropriate conjunctions.

1 TV advertising works very well. It is expensive.

2 Some advertisements have to be aired after nine o'clock. Most children are in bed by that time.

3 Good sales are often linked to good advertising. Bad sales are not often linked to bad advertising.

4 You can advertise alcohol on television. You can advertise smoking on billboards.

5 This advertising campaign has been really popular. Viewing figures are beginning to drop off a bit.

6 Why bother advertising at all. Word of mouth can be pretty strong.

7 We could call them and complain. We could write a letter.

8 I'll buy that brand. I see a cheaper one.

D Complete the gaps with appropriate vocabulary.

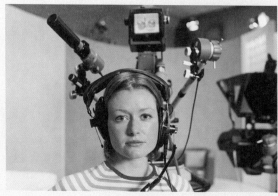

1   The television station was _____ requests to show the programme again.

2   The staff need to _____ management.

3   We gave up our train tickets _____ $200.

4   I am _____ the company's logo.

5   Food _____ in the ability of children to concentrate.

6   The football team is _____ a brand of beer.

7   She gets $500 dollars _____ every sale over $2000 that she makes.

8   She is the perfect _____ how not to behave at a party.

9   This ad will really _____ the young-at-heart.

10 Good restaurants in this area are _____, really.

11 I don't want him _____ those kind of people.

12 These pronunciation difficulties are _____ Chinese students.

13 I don't care where we go for dinner, it's _____ you.

14 We need _____ quite carefully before we make any more decisions.

15 Even after hours of debating it, I still couldn't _____ him.

16 Smoking is _____ her poor health.

17 Extra guests are permitted to stay _____ the hotel manager.

E Some of the conjunctions used below are incorrect. Write the correct one. Sometimes more than one conjunction is possible.

1   I saw Melita at the library or I didn't see her boyfriend. _____

2   She appears to be extremely patient for kind. _____

3   I'll go to France nor Spain in the next summer break. _____

4   He was running late so I picked him up from work. _____

5   I haven't been there yet but I plan to go as soon as possible. _____

6   Until you were sleeping, the cat got out of the house. _____

7   After I finish this, I'll start the project. _____

8   He won the race though he hadn't trained. _____

9   Although we go there, I want to visit the famous lake. _____

10 Don't leave in case we have an emergency. _____

F Rank the criteria below in terms of importance to you when buying a product or service. Write an example of a product after each criterion.

ranking	criterion	product or service
_____	value for money	_____
_____	style	_____
_____	reliability	_____
_____	size	_____
_____	price	_____
_____	quality	_____
_____	functionality	_____

G Write a paragraph referring to a product you own or would like to own and explain how it justifies your ranking in Exercise F.

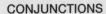

Language Reference

CONJUNCTIONS

We use conjunctions to join phrases or clauses. They are used to signal a connection between the meanings of the two clauses or phrases. Conjunctions are usually divided into two categories: co-coordinating conjunctions and subordinating conjunctions.

Co-ordinating conjunctions connect similar elements in a sentence, such as nouns, adjectives, and verbs, depending on the meaning. They are also the conjunctions used to join independent clauses together. These include 'and', 'but', 'or', 'for', 'nor', 'yet' and 'so'.

Subordinating conjunctions introduce dependent clauses, also known as adverb clauses. Examples are 'because', 'since', 'when', 'while', 'before', 'after', 'until', 'although', 'though', 'whereas', 'if', 'in case', and 'unless'.

In clauses joined with co-ordinating conjunctions, words which repeat ideas can be left out.
We liked the advertisement but thought the music was well-suited. ('we' is left out)

'And' is used to show addition.
He studies in the mornings, and he teaches in the afternoons.

'But' shows contrast.
They got married, but decided not to have children.

'Or' gives a choice.
I can go online, or I can go to the library.

'For' means 'because' but is more formal.
They survived, for they were strong.

'Nor' shows denial and requires inversion of verb and subject.
The lawyer said there was no evidence, nor was there proof.

'Yet' means despite the circumstances.
They had prepared, yet they were nervous.

'So' shows consequence.
We were very late, so we took a taxi to the station.

'Because' and 'since' are used to show reason / cause and effect.
She was angry because he had forgotten to call.
Since you don't like pepper, we'll leave it out.

'When', 'while', 'before', 'after' and 'until' show time.
We ate out every night when we were in Singapore.
Don't leave before phoning your mother.
He is staying until the party is over.

'Although', 'though' and 'whereas' show contrast.
Although we are nearly finished, we still have more to do.
I like red wine whereas my partner likes white wine.

'If', 'in case', and 'unless' indicate condition.
If you email me, I'll send you the file.
You don't have to log on again unless you have signed out.

In subordinate clauses, a pronoun followed by the verb 'to be' can be left out after 'if', 'when', 'while', 'until', 'once', 'unless' and 'although'.
We like music in advertising if it is well-suited.
We like music in advertising if well-suited.

Also, many conjunctions such as 'after', 'before', 'since', 'when', 'while', 'whenever', 'once', and 'until', can be followed by an '-ing' form instead of a clause.
I always want the latest mobile phone after I have watched the new advertisements.
I always want the latest mobile phone after watching new advertisements.

Commas are important to separate clauses joined by conjunctions in certain cases. In the case of Co-ordinating conjunctions, use a comma before the conjunction. When using subordinating conjunctions, use a comma to separate the clauses only when the subordinate clause comes first.

The ad sales were down, but the magazine went ahead with publication.
Before we shoot an ad for television, we audition many people.

The environment

After this unit, you should be able to ...

- Read about global warming
- Read about endangered species
- Write a brief summary of a process
- Understand and use different forms of the conditional
- Listen to lectures and radio programmes and take notes
- Design a leaflet
- Describe a diagram

A Describe the environment of your country to a fellow student. Explain what life in that country is like. Listen to each other's descriptions. Discuss differences and similarities.

B Compare and contrast the two pictures saying what problems you think they illustrate.

C If you had to describe in detail what 'paradise' would be for you, what would you say? Would it have animals? Which ones? What would the temperature, food, architecture and people be like?

Speaking and Reading

A What are some of the challenges facing our environment today? Choose from the list below and add some more of your own.

overpopulation
not enough green land
land erosion
water level
animal extinction
air quality

B Read the titles of some newspaper and magazine articles below. Explain what they mean in your own words.

a   Burning CO 2 may solve the problem

b   Glaciers heading for point of no return

c   Climate change: The Great Atlantic Shutdown

d   Climate blamed for animal extinction

e   Wild weather scares the Earth

f   Whales move north as oceans warm

g   Climate change is more serious than the threat of terrorism

h   Petrol, we can't live with it and we can't live without it

C How much do scientists expect the world's temperature to rise in the next 100 years? Read the article to check.

The Earth has got warmer by about one degree in the past 100 years, which seems to be faster than in previous centuries. In the Polar Regions temperatures have risen by two degrees in the same period. Even more amazingly, in some parts of Alaska, temperatures appear to have risen by more than ten degrees in the last thirty years. The questions are 'why' and 'how'? It could be that the Earth is getting warmer by itself, but scientists are convinced that human activities are helping to make it warmer. A warmer Earth could lead to changes in rain fall, the level of the sea may rise dangerously, and our plants and wildlife will suffer. If temperatures were to rise above normal for a few days it would not be a problem or anything to worry about. But if they continued to rise over a longer period then the Earth may experience problems which, depending on the country or area, could be catastrophic.

Scientists expect the global temperature to increase by two to six degrees Celsius during the next century. As numbers, these don't represent much but this increase could bring irreversible changes to our climate. If we go back to the last Ice Age (18,000 years ago) the temperature was only four degrees cooler than what it is today and back then glaciers covered much of North America. If the climate changes, this may also change the things we depend on. For example, it may change the level of our oceans and the places where we can plant our crops. It may also include changes in the air we breathe and the water we drink. So what exactly might happen?

Scientists don't really know for sure. Some temperature changes will benefit some very cold regions like Canada and Siberia where they would gladly welcome warmer temperatures that would make their days and nights more comfortable. This would allow them to grow more crops. But overall, the continuing global warming will result in more problems than benefits. People's health is already feeling the impact of the rise in temperatures. Conditions like heat stress, skin cancer and other related problems are caused by very warm temperatures. The world's habitats and ecosystems are affected, too. They depend on a balance of rainfall, soil type and temperature in order to survive. The most minimal change in any of these may result in irreversible alterations. If further climate change occurs as predicted, plants and animals may not be able to react quickly enough to survive.

Global warming is not affecting just one part of the world. All the continents have already witnessed and experienced phenomena directly associated with the rise in the Earth's temperature. In Australia, coral reefs are dying very fast. In fact, experts predict that the Great Barrier Reef will be dead within thirty years. The United Kingdom is experiencing very strong storms and floods more frequently than in the past. Southern Europe was ravaged by hundreds of wildfires destroying a huge part of its forests. The USA has experienced the effects of very long droughts and heat waves which are responsible for hundreds of deaths and disastrous crop failures. Indonesia has had to suffer from droughts, crop failure and forest fires. Antarctica continues to melt with temperatures having risen 2.5 degrees Celsius since the 1940s. Coastal flooding in Bangladesh has become more and more common killing thousands of people. Experts believe that if the sea level in this part of the world went up by just one metre, Bangladesh would lose 17.5% of its land causing major problems such as overpopulation in other areas.

D Read the text again and answer the questions.

1 Why is it amazing that temperatures in Alaska appear to have risen by more than ten degrees in the last thirty years?

2 Is human activity believed to be the only cause of this?

3 What could be some of the effects of global warming?

4 What physical affects could global warming have on humans?

5 Why would habitats and ecosystems be destroyed?

6 Which word from the text means a very rapidly moving forest fire?

7 What has killed many people recently in the USA?

8 What is a particular threat in the Far East?

E Look at the picture below. Describe to your partner what is happening in it, and what the environmental phenomenon is.

F Draw up a list of natural disasters that have happened recently. You may need to do some research. List where they occurred and what their effect was. Where are they more likely to occur? Why is that, do you think? Discuss with fellow students. At the end present your disasters in class and tell your fellow students what you know about them.

Homework Look back at the newspaper headings in Exercise B. Choose one and prepare a short 200-word newspaper article about the subject. Give evidence to support your ideas.

A Look at the pictures below. Which types of pollution do they illustrate? Write the types under the pictures.

_____ _____

_____ _____

B Read the list of consequences of pollution. Which do you think are the most serious? Why?

1   skin rash
2   cough
3   bronchitis
4   longer days
5   eye irritation
6   heart problems
7   headaches
8   erosion
9   miscarriages
10 birth defects
11 flooding
12 learning difficulties
13 breakdown of the ozone layer
14 death to animal life
15 death to plant life
16 car problems
17 communication problems
18 bad air
19 contamination
20 breakdown of the food chain

 C You are going to listen to a lecture on pollution. Circle the words you think you may hear. Then listen to check your answers.

lecture	☐
acid rain	☐
effects	☐
fog	☐
snow	☐
theme	☐
smog	☐
transferred	☐
invisible	☐
chemicals	☐
particles	☐
exuded	☐
relative	☐
source	☐
analysis	☐
sulphur dioxide	☐
traced	☐
superlative	☐
radically	☐
nitrogen oxide	☐
environment	☐
creatures	☐
skeletal structure	☐
fossil fuels	☐
mild forms	☐
food chain	☐
consternation	☐
concentrations	☐
urban	☐
expend	☐
indigenous	☐
make up	☐
pre-industrial society	☐
attempting	☐
minimise	☐

D Look at the outline of the lecture. Listen again and take notes.

Title: _____

I   What is Acid Rain?

II How does acid deposit?

    A   _____

    B   _____

    C   _____

III What causes acid depositions?

    A   _____

    B   _____

IV What effects do acid deposits have on the environment?

    A   _____

    B   _____

E Combine the words you ticked in Exercise C with the notes you took in Exercise D and write 5 or 6 sentences based on what you heard in the lecture.

F Look back at the words that you didn't tick in Exercise C. Which words do you not know? See if you can tell your partner what the words they don't know mean.

G The pictures below illustrate another kind of pollution. Answer the questions.

a   Study the images. What do you think this type of pollution is?

b   Can you give other examples of this?

c   If it doesn't really harm us, why is it considered a problem?

d   How is it associated with publicity and communication?

Reading and Speaking

A What does the phrase 'endangered animals' mean? Who or what are they in danger from? What reasons would anyone have for putting the lives of animals in danger? Can you name any endangered species?

B Human beings consume and use many products that are of animal origin. Can you make a list of them? Use these categories to help you.

Things we wear	Food	Luxury items	Decorative items

C Read the article. Which endangered species are mentioned?

A species is considered 'endangered' if it is threatened with extinction throughout all or in a very large part of its habitat. A species is considered 'threatened' if it is likely to become endangered in the future. A species can also be called a species of 'special concern' when, even though it is not endangered or threatened, there are not many of them in an area. This labeling helps start opportune campaigns to protect animals.

All continents have their own species that are either endangered or threatened—some more than others because of the characteristics of the environment. In North America man is the bald eagle's main enemy. During Winter periods the bald eagle requires a very large home making it very vulnerable to habitat destruction by man. Environmental problems have also been the main cause of the disappearance of the bald eagle, pollution being the most serious. These animals need to feed on the fish in rivers which are often contaminated with pesticides. This is also the problem faced by other North American animals such as the falcon and the Californian condor of which there are less than 50 in existence.

Europe, having very high mountains, is the home of one of these endangered species, the ibex. These are very large mountain goats. These impressive animals, that have been known to jump lengths of up to 40 feet, are endangered because man hunts them for game and sport: hunters consider it a challenge to find them in such remote locations. As with ibexes, musk oxen, also found in Europe, are in danger because of hunting.

Oceania has two main animals that are considered endangered. One of these is the rare takahe, a bird that does not fly. It is found in New Zealand. This bird was considered extinct in the 1800s but in the late 1940s several were rediscovered making this species extremely rare. They have become endangered for two main reasons. Firstly, because of construction near their habitat and secondly, because of their inability to fly which has made them easy to catch and kill. The other endangered animal from Oceania is far more popular with the public. It is the koala bear with its beautiful fur. Koalas have become endangered precisely because of their soft fur which is used in the fashion industry.

South America has a large variety of birds. It is not surprising that one of its most endangered species is the colourful (red, blue and yellow) scarlet macaw. It is famous not only because of its colourful body but also because it has the incredible ability to mimic human sound. It is also one of the most easily trained of all birds. It is not surprising that this bird has become endangered due to the overwhelming demand for its colourful feathers in the fashion industry. Its ability to mimic sounds and learn tricks has also made it very appealing as a pet.

South America is also the home of one of the strangest looking animals, the anteater. This animal has many limitations with habitat and food. It lives in forests, swampy areas and plains. It eats only insects and only gives birth to one baby at a time. It is endangered due to the constant loss of forest area and the fact that it has a very low reproduction rate.

D Read the article again and answer the questions.

1 Which explanations does the article give as to why animals become 'endangered species'?

2 How can the land in which the animals live make them vulnerable? Give examples.

3 What role does 'man' play in this?

4 Define these words and phrases from the article.

a likely to become _____

b reproduction rate _____

c remote _____

d mimic _____

e overwhelming demand _____

f faced by _____

g a challenge _____

h appealing _____

i game _____

j opportune _____

5 How do you think that labeling animals as 'endangered' 'threatened' or 'of concern' helps protect them? How does the government use this information?

6 Why does the fact that people like macaws as pets put this species in danger?

7 How do you think the takahe disappeared for such a long time and then reappeared?

8 How can an animal's diet make it vulnerable?

E Habitat destruction is the greatest threat to species all over the world. Humans have altered, degraded, and destroyed habitats in so many different ways. The following are examples of activities that destroy animal habitats. Match the activities on the left with the damage they do on the right. Often more than one answer is possible.

_____ logging

_____ agriculture

_____ housing development

_____ mining

_____ wood production

_____ water development such as dams

_____ water separation for human use

_____ industrial pollution

_____ over fishing

a dries up vegetation along rivers leaving animals with insufficient water

b changes the water flow and temperature of the rivers

c forces animals to relocate which puts them in danger with other animals

d changes the characteristics of the land

e releases harmful chemicals destroying the food chain and causing reproductive problems

f causes chemicals to contaminate waters

g destroys forests

h clears complete areas leaving animals defenseless

i animals are killed faster than they can reproduce

j destroys forests

Homework Research another endangered species and present the information to the class.

Grammar

A Match the halves of these famous quotations. Do you agree with them?

1   If you stick to an idea,   ☐   ☐   a   the rich would have kept it all to themselves.

2   If you can imagine it,   ☐   ☐   b   you can achieve it.

3   If success is not on your own terms,   ☐   ☐   c   it's not real.

4   If you only do what you know,   ☐   ☐   d   spring would not be pleasant.

5   If we had no winter,   ☐   ☐   e   you never do very much.

6   If hard work were such a wonderful thing,   ☐   ☐   f   it might not all work, but some of it will.

7   If we don't change,   ☐   ☐   g   we don't grow.

What structures do the quotations use and why? Read the Language Reference on page 32 to check your answers.

B Complete the gaps with appropriate forms of the verbs in brackets.

1   If you _____ (mix) NO and water, you _____ (get) nitric acid.

2   If you _____ (try) to export ivory, you _____ (be) arrested.

3   If the United Nations _____ (not pass) this new resolution, it _____ (mean) big trouble for the environment.

4   If petrol _____ (be) more expensive, it _____ (cut) the number of cars on the road.

5   If it _____ (be) possible to reduce the amount of greenhouse gases in the atmosphere, the greenhouse affect _____ (be) reversed.

6   If scientists _____ (not discovered) the hole in the ozone layer all those years ago, things _____ (be) worse today than they already are.

7   If we _____ (not be) careful, there _____ (be) anything to leave our children.

8   If we _____ (continue) to burn fossil fuels at this rate, resources _____ (run) out by the end of the century.

9   If the ice caps _____ (melt), Bournemouth, Brighton, New York and Sydney _____ (disappear).

10   If all governments _____ (sign) the new treaty, greenhouse gases _____ (reduce).

C Connect the ideas by writing one sentence using one of the conditionals. The first one has been done for you.

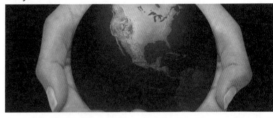

1   The animals didn't leave. The hurricane arrived all of a sudden.

> ■ **EXAMPLE**
>
> *If the animals had known the hurricane was coming, they would have left.*

2   In South America they did not protect the macaw well enough. The bird is now an endangered species.

3   The sea level rose in Indonesia. They experienced terrible floods.

4   The government didn't pass the new protection law. The elephants were hunted and killed.

5   The protest leader went alone. Nobody paid attention to her.

6   The duck got stuck in one of the pipes. There was a lot of garbage in the water.

D Use the words given and show how likely you think these things are by choosing the correct conditional form.

1 If / stop using aerosols / reduce CO2 emissions
2 If / don't stop burning fossil fuels / greenhouse effect get worse
3 If / ivory poaching continue / elephants become extinct
4 If / be president of the USA / introduce new carbon emission laws
5 If / the Prime Minister be re-elected / introduce new environmental policies
6 If / we stop using cars / greenhouse effect slow down
7 If / tigers be made protected species / we stop their extinction
8 If / sailors not shoot the dodo / not be extinct
9 If / governments want to / save the environment
10 If / sea level / rise / Indonesia / suffer

E Work with a partner. Use conditional verb forms.

> **EXAMPLE**
>
> Threaten to tell the teacher that your partner is copying:
> *If you copy from my paper again, I will tell the teacher.*

1 Convince a fellow student to buy your watch
2 Go to a fellow student and finish this sentence after 'If I were you …
3 Ask a fellow student something about a scientific process. 'What happens if …'

4 Warn a fellow student about something.
5 Give your teacher an excuse for being late.
6 Threaten the student next to you.
7 Tell a fellow student something you regret from your past.
8 Negotiate changing seats with a fellow student.

F Express your opinions about endangered animals or global warming, using conditional verb forms.

1 Criticise the use of radioactive materials.
2 Warn the government about protecting the koala.
3 Make a prediction about sea levels.
4 Write something that is very likely to happen in the Arctic.
5 Blame one particular company for something.
6 Describe how different life would be if there was no global warming.

G Write several sentences for each idea.

1 Write about how life would have been different if the Industrial Revolution hadn't happened?
2 Who would you blame for the endangered species if not man?
3 How will animals survive without human intervention?
4 What might the future be like for the following animals if global warming continues?
   a penguins   d the bald eagle
   b tigers   e seals
   c dogs   f whale
5 Which countries won't even be populated if the Earth warms up?

Listening and Writing

A What items can be found in most household rubbish? Will any of these things be re-used? List the contents of a rubbish bag.

B Listen to a radio programme. What is recycling? How does it work? What is the difference between recycling and re-using?

C Listen again and answer the questions.

1 What do these numbers refer to?

    a   6,000,000

    _____

    b   12,000,000,000

    _____

    c   2

    _____

    d   25,000,000

    _____

2 Where does most household waste go?

_____

3 What are some examples of household waste?

_____

4 How does landfill threaten the environment?

_____

_____

5 How can you be 'green' whilst shopping?

_____

_____

6 How is the rest of our rubbish disposed of?

_____

7 Does recycling waste energy?

_____

_____

8 What is better than recycling?

_____

9 What are landfills?

_____

10 What can we do with our plastic bags?

_____

D Complete these sentences.

1 It would save trees if, … _____

2 If we burnt more waste, … _____

3 If you go to the supermarket, … _____

4 If everybody used reusable nappies, … _____

5 If more things were re-used, … _____

6 If you make a new tin can, … _____

7 If we ate less tinned food, … _____

8 If we want to reduce the greenhouse effect, … _____

9 If everybody did just one thing, … _____

10 If we all worked together, … _____

E Complete the table using the items from the list.

	magazines		folders with metal hangers
	paper with food stains		catalogues
	food tins		food packaging
	plastic cups		newspapers
	binders		photos
	typing paper		envelopes with plastic windows
	memos		motor oil cans
	towels		cash register receipts
	mobile phone batteries		letterhead paper
	blankets		cardboard boxes
	jars		drinks cans

can be recycled		cannot be recycled	
work / school	home	work / school	home

F In groups make a list of all the items you have in your pockets, bags and on your desks. Include the clothes you are wearing. Divide the items into two groups: things that can be recycled and things that cannot be recycled.

a   How many things in total cannot be recycled?

b   How many things in total can be recycled?

c   How many can be re-used?

d   Which of these products can you change for things that can be recycled?

e   Walk around the classroom to see what kind of items your classmates have.

G Using the information given in the radio programme in Exercise B and all the information from the previous exercises, design a leaflet to encourage …

a   families to recycle

b   a specific company to recycle

c   your country's government to recycle.

d   protection of endangered species

e   reduction in pollution

f   people to help slow down global warming

Reading and Writing

A Read an article about the 'greenhouse effect'. Use the information from the text to complete the diagram below.

The Earth receives most of its energy from the sun in the form of radiation. This radiation is of a special type called 'electromagnetic radiation' with small amounts of infrared (IR) and ultraviolet (UV). The incoming solar energy has a very short wavelength which passes through the atmospheric gases to reach the surface of the Earth in the form of light. The Earth's surface absorbs this energy and releases it back into the atmosphere as infrared radiation in the form of heat. Some of it goes back into space. Some of the IR radiation emitted by the Earth is then absorbed by gases found in the atmosphere that re-emit the energy back to the Earth's surface in the form of heat. There are three gases found in our atmosphere carbon dioxide, methane, and water which contribute to the greenhouse effect. These gases absorb the infrared radiation and radiate the energy again in the form of heat back towards the Earth's surface, causing it to warm up and producing the greenhouse effect.

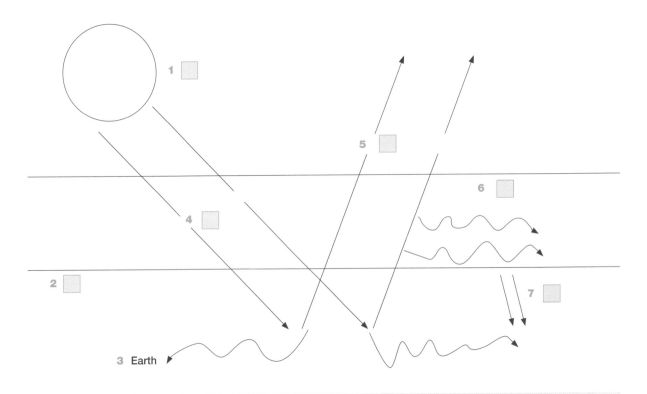

3 Earth

a	some greenhouse gases absorb the heat	d	atmosphere
b	the Sun	e	atmosphere and earth reflect heat back
c	the greenhouse gases heat up the earth	f	sun sends heat to the earth

B Practise explaining the process.

C Using the following information create a pie chart and write a paragraph to accompany it, explaining the data. Use the text in Exercise A as an example.

> Sources of CO2 Emissions in the World in 2005. (million metric tons)   World total : 23,284.2

Oceania : 383.9

Sub-Saharan Africa : 467.1

Central America & Caribbean : 484.8

North America : 6,202.3

Middle East & N. Africa : 1,455.3

Asia (excluding Middle East) : 7,402.8

Europe: 6,156.9

South America: 731.1

D Use a diagram to illustrate the information below. Then write three paragraphs to accompany your diagram.

> 236 million tons of rubbish produced - 90 million tons recycled.

35 paper	11 plastics	6 wood
12 food	8 metals	5 glass
12 garden waste	7 leather, textiles	4 other

E We send greenhouse gases into the air when we do these things. In groups find out how many of you do these things and how much time do you spend on them each day. Create a chart or diagram to illustrate how much greenhouse gas you are emitting. Be creative in your presentation and description.

use a hair dryer	drive a car
watch TV	use the air conditioner
play video games	use the dishwasher
microwave a meal	turn on a light

F Look at the information about the numbers of endangered species in the USA. Write ten questions based on the table.

	1980	2000
mammals	32	65
birds	55	76
reptiles	12	14
amphibians	5	15
fish	31	70

> **■ EXAMPLE**
>
> *How many more species of mammals were endangered in 1980 than reptiles?*

G Get a fellow student to answer your questions.

H Pick a subject that really interests you. This could be one of the subjects of this unit, or it could be something completely different. Do some research and draw a graph illustrating interesting information or showing important developments. Put data in and around the graph, and then perform the tasks described below.

a Discuss your graph with a fellow student in which you discuss the data, its repercussions and developments. Your partner must ask questions for clarification, and you may need to do more research to find out what they want to know.

b Incorporate the results of your discussion and further research and present the graph to the class. Describe the information, describe developments and speculate about what could happen and what should happen to change or improve things.

> **Homework**

Write a 300-word report on the subject of endangered species. Try to convince people of the seriousness of the situation and picture some developments for the future. Suggest actions that need to be undertaken, and what people should be stopped from doing. Bring your report to class for peer correction.

Language Practice

A
Make sentences that best combine the following ideas.

1   John and Pattie got stuck on the highway. There was a terrible accident ahead of them.

_____
_____
_____

2   Astrid missed the party last night. She never got the invitation in the mail.

_____
_____

3   Claudia didn't pay her electricity bill. The company cut her off this morning.

_____
_____

4   Laura went to class this morning. There was no class because it was a national holiday.

_____
_____
_____

5   Melito got to the game late. They changed the time from 7 to 5.

_____
_____

6   Paula got married to Robert last week. She just found out he drinks too much.

_____
_____

7   They gave away two new cars at the premiere last night. Estevan and Melissa didn't go.

_____
_____

8   Marietta and Luca didn't do their homework. The teacher assigned the work last Tuesday and they were both absent.

_____
_____
_____

B
Answer the questions using one of the conditional verb forms.

What would happen if ...

1   dogs could talk to their owners?

2   there were no gun control laws in the USA?

3   you could speak English perfectly?

4   solar energy were our only source?

5   you could be another person?

6   we could fix our own cars?

7   you could have all the money you needed?

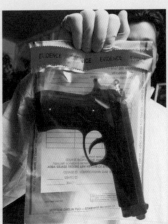

C Match the halves to best complete the sentences.

1 If the bald eagle continues to disappear, ☐
2 If he studied at a different time, ☐
3 If you need to change your life, ☐
4 If it hadn't turned out as it did, ☐
5 If life gives you lemons, ☐
6 If there is a will, ☐
7 If you see her, ☐
8 If I were you, ☐
9 If he had paid more attention to his wife, ☐
10 Most of his problems could have been resolved, ☐

☐ a   tell her I miss her terribly.
☐ b   we would be in a better hotel right now.
☐ c   he would not get so distracted.
☐ d   she wouldn't have left him.
☐ e   there is a way.
☐ f   make lemonade.
☐ g   a good place to start is with your job.
☐ h   the American symbol will be lost.
☐ i   if he had confided in his friends.
☐ j   I would just tell him 'goodbye'.

D Fill the gaps.

1 If I hadn't called the police, the thief _____ away.

2 Had they not protected their home, the hurricane _____ it.

3 People don't realise that if they don't take care of their bodies, they _____ to get sick.

4 I know now that if I want to earn more money, I _____ to get a better degree.

5 If you pressure me any harder, I _____ tomorrow.

6 My friend thinks that you can only find a good wife, if you _____ to church.

7 Wouldn't life be wonderful if we _____ better communication skills!

8 I would be nicer to him if he _____ so arrogant.

9 You are never going to be anybody in life if you _____ that way!

10 Why didn't you call him if you _____ he was in trouble?

E Go online to find out more information about global warming. Write up a 300-word report, in which you must try to convince people of the seriousness of the situation and picture some developments for the future. Suggest actions that need to be undertaken, and what people should be stopped from doing.

CONDITIONAL VERB FORMS

Conditional sentences refer to situations that are real, predictions, and situations that are impossible or imaginative. There are four types of conditionals: type 0, 1, 2 and 3.

Type	IF clause	CONDITIONAL clause	Example	Use
0	'If' + present	present	• If you need to change your money, you go to a bank.	• to express general truths. • to express something that basically always happens • to express a scientific fact
1	'If' + present	future	• If I see her, I'll tell her you called. • If you come by here again, I will call the police.	• to express something that is possible and also very likely to happen • to express a warning or threat
2	'If' + past	'would' + bare infinitive	• If he studied more, he would be an excellent student. • If I got an invitation, I would go with you for sure.	• to express something that is not real • to express something that is impossible or contrary to facts
3	'If' + past perfect	'would' + 'have'+ past participle	• If she hadn't memorised the verbs, she wouldn't have passed that grammar test.	• to speculate about past events • to express how things might have happened in another way • to express imaginative ideas about things which are impossible

Sometimes we can also use the 3rd Conditional to express regret about something, or anger towards something or someone.

If you hadn't driven so fast, we wouldn't have had the accident.

If he hadn't lied to me, I wouldn't have said those bad things to him.

I would have helped you if you had asked me politely.

Some other forms of the 1st, 2nd and 3rd Conditionals can be a bit confusing but nonetheless very functional and necessary for every day conversations and situations.

1st Conditional

1) 'If' + present   imperative
If you pass by the store, get me a packet of crisps.

2) 'If' + present   present continous
If the bus doesn't come on time today, we're staying home.

3) 'If' + present   'going to'
If Dad remembers , we are going to see a baseball game this afternoon.

2nd Conditional

1) 'If' + 'were' + infinitive   'would'
If the temperature were to rise too much the Earth would be in terrible danger.

2) 'Were' + subject   'would'
Were he nicer to me, I would be nicer to him.

3rd Conditional

'Had' + subject + past participle (no use of 'if')
Had I known he was her father, I would never have told him what she did.

What's in the news?

After this unit, you should be able to ...

- Listen for gist and details
- Work with media vocabulary
- Use prepositions
- Debate media censorship
- Create and use compound nouns
- Write newspaper headlines and short reports

A Which types of media do you use most often in daily life? Are all of the media you want to use available in your country? Which ones are the most popular among your peers?

B What are the main news stories at the moment? What have been the major stories so far this year? Do you feel they are all newsworthy?

C Are there big differences between newspapers in your country and where you are studying? Look at the newspapers your teacher gives you and make comparisons.

Listening and Speaking

A Complete the table below with examples of the two different kinds of media. Compare your table with another pair and report back to the class.

Print media	Broadcast media

 B You are going to hear part of a radio show about the death of John Packwell, a media tycoon. Complete the sentences.

1 The hospital ...
   a   doesn't know the cause of death
   b   may know the cause of death
   c   does know the cause of death

2 The dead man ...
   a   often complained about his health
   b   complained about his health that day
   c   was fit and healthy

3 At the Packwell Corporation ...
   a   the building is ultra-conservative
   b   the people are ultra-conservative
   c   the people who read their papers are conservative

4 Since the incident with the chicken, Max Pelet ...
   a   has had trouble standing
   b   has had trouble with his career
   c   has had trouble with his reputation

5 The new boss is likely to be ...
   a   appointed from another organisation
   b   appointed from Packwell's family
   c   promoted from within the corporation

6 The radio show's anchor suggests that ...
   a   people will miss Packwell badly
   b   people will not be very upset about Packwell's death
   c   people will falsely claim to miss Packwell badly

7 Following the death of John Packwell ...
   a   people will have a better night's sleep
   b   people will have a worse night's sleep
   c   people will be less worried

8 The news reporter ...
   a   thinks Packwell may have been murdered
   b   refuses to consider the possibility of murder
   c   thinks Packwell wasn't murdered

C Choose the correct word to complete these sentences.

		A		B	
1	Sounds like we're in for some bad _____.	A	weather	B	whether
2	The death of the media mogul was _____.	A	renounced	B	announced
3	He was _____ to hospital.	A	omitted	B	admitted
4	Packwell had media _____ everywhere.	A	interesting	B	interests
5	This is going to give _____ to speculation.	A	raise	B	rise
6	I tend to _____ leftist politicians.	A	import	B	support
7	It is _____ that a woman will ever take over.	A	likely	B	unlikely
8	Could you _____ that please?	A	repeat	B	receive
9	That comment is somewhat _____!	A	insensitive	B	sensible
10	It will be good without him _____ down our necks.	A	breezing	B	breathing

D The following words appeared in the recording. Match the words to their definitions.

1	mogul ▣	▣ a	prepared for promotion
2	tycoon ▣	▣ b	make clearer by giving information
3	admitted ▣	▣ c	very successful business person
4	repercussions ▣	▣ d	person who takes over
5	interests ▣	▣ e	guesses
6	speculation ▣	▣ f	things you have invested in
7	elaborate ▣	▣ g	allowed to enter a place
8	successor ▣	▣ h	consequences
9	groomed ▣	▣ i	get rid of, let fall
10	shed ▣	▣ j	important media personality

E What do the underlined expressions mean?

1 We're going live with some <u>breaking news</u>.

_____

2 He's <u>a bit of</u> a pessimist.

_____

3 <u>Once again</u>, this is going to have repercussions.

_____

4 I've <u>taken an active interest</u> in these matters.

_____

5 My <u>standing</u> has suffered in this scandal.

_____

6 Is this a typical case of <u>foul play</u>?

_____

7 I <u>couldn't possibly</u> speculate.

_____

F Listen to the interview on media ownership. Which of these opinions are given by each speaker. Write J (for Jennifer), W (for Wal) or B (for Both).

1 Media ownership by a small group of companies is not a good thing. _____

2 Businesses should be allowed to develop naturally. _____

3 Competition is beneficial to the market. _____

4 The benefit of the media for society has decreased over time. _____

5 There are many opportunities for people to express themselves through the media. _____

6 Large conglomerates find it hard to deal with the power they have. _____

7 There is enormous variety and diversity in the media. _____

8 Ownership of the distribution channels is central to the issue of media power. _____

G Discuss the questions. Then exchange your ideas with other pairs.
Report back to the class. Can you reach agreement?

1 Should individuals be allowed to own newspapers or TV stations?

2 Can these individuals be politicians?

3 Is it better if governments control the media?

4 Is it possible for government-owned media to criticise the government?

5 Should the media endorse one political party over another?

6 Should the media simply report news, or should it be allowed to influence news?

Reading and Grammar

A Discuss the questions.

1 Do you think the media generally handles disasters sensitively?

2 Is it right to show pictures of people who have died? Where do you draw the line?

3 Can you think of times when the reporting of disasters has had a positive outcome?

B Read the newspaper report. Fill the gaps with an appropriate preposition.

Killer Wave Drowns Asia

(1) _____ 8 o'clock local time (2) _____ 26 December 2004, the world changed for tens of thousands living (3) _____ the Indian Ocean rim. Many, indeed, would never see another sunrise. An earthquake measuring nine on the Richter Scale exploded (4) _____ the ocean (5) _____ the coast of Sumatra, Indonesia's largest island; the shock waves igniting a tsunami which sped (6) _____ the ocean. 48 hours after the initial catastrophe, people still did not know what the death toll was. It now stands at approximately 250,000.

In Sumatra itself, the province of Aceh was flooded, but the disaster wasn't just a local one. A wall of water (7) _____ 10 metres high smashed (8) _____ the coasts of India, Thailand, Sri Lanka, the Maldive Islands, the Andaman and Nicobar Islands, Burma, Bangladesh and Malaysia. By the morning, the tsunami had travelled over 7,000 kilometres and was battering Somalia and

Kenya in East Africa. The largest earthquake in 40 years had become the biggest natural disaster that the United Nations had ever had to deal (9) _____.

So, what is a tsunami? It's often called a tidal wave though this is a misnomer since the wave has nothing to do with tides. It's a devastating ocean wave usually caused by a submarine earthquake, though sometimes the result of a submarine landslide or volcanic eruption. Often, the first sign of approaching catastrophe is the water receding and exposing the shallow sea floor. Such an occurrence, (10) _____ Lisbon, Portugal, on 1 November, 1755, attracted many curious people to the bay floor, most of whom were drowned by the wave that arrived only minutes later. Perhaps the most destructive tsunami was the one that occurred (11) _____ 1703 at Awa, Japan, killing more than 100,000 people. The spectacular underwater volcanic explosions that obliterated Krakatau Island, again in Indonesia, on 26 and 27 August, 1883, created waves as high as 35 metres (12) _____ many Indian Ocean localities, killing more than 36,000 people. For a while people thought that the tsunami devastation of 2004 had yet to reach the levels of 1703 or 1883. The reality of it would become apparent all too soon and both were to be eclipsed by the time the final death toll was known.

1	a At	b In	c On
2	a at	b in	c on
3	a at	b around	c on
4	a beneath	b in	c down
5	a off	b in	c on
6	a at	b towards	c across

7	a at	b up to	c onto
8	a up to	b into	c onto
9	a out	b in	c with
10	a at	b in	c on
11	a at	b in	c on
12	a at	b in	c on

C Are the following statements True or False?

1 **T F** The disaster struck at 8:00 am GMT.
2 **T F** Sumatra is an island in the Indian Ocean.
3 **T F** A tsunami can fly.
4 **T F** For the UN, this was the worst disaster in 40 years.
5 **T F** A tsunami is another name for a very large tidal wave.
6 **T F** A tsunami is caused by a massive underwater disturbance.
7 **T F** In 1755, most of the people who died were tourists.
8 **T F** The earthquake at Awa, Japan, caused the worst tsunami.
9 **T F** The Krakatau waves were higher than those from the Sumatra quake.
10 **T F** The final death toll from the Sumatra disaster has never become known.

D Some of the following sentences contain preposition errors. Tick (✓) the correct sentences. If you think the preposition is wrong, write the correct preposition.

1 The news programming on Channel 9 is best.

2 Have you seen the new Spielberg film? It's playing in the Odeon.

3 Why don't you look the word up in the dictionary?

4 The BBC HQ is at London.

5 Have you seen that photo on the front page?

6 I couldn't bear to watch the images in the screen.

7 John's at the publisher's.

8 The library at Levelly Crescent is excellent.

E

Is there such a thing as 'good news' or is news always bad? Most of what we see on our TV screens seems to be bad news. Should the media report good news, too? Is bad news used as a tool to keep people subdued and afraid? Have a debate about the statement 'Good News is Bad News'.

Reading

A Read the quotations and match them with the photographs. Working with a fellow-student, explain your choices. What are they talking about?

a ☐
b ☐
c ☐
d ☐
e ☐

a For us it is an excellent instrument to stay in touch with the people. As you will appreciate, people like reading the innermost thoughts of their favourite representatives. It's also a tool which we use to keep people informed, and bring our work closer to people.

c I can't make up my mind about this new medium. What on earth can bring any person to sharing their most personal thoughts with, well, basically anybody anywhere. Is there no such thing as privacy anymore? And aren't most of these things totally uninteresting?

b As an organisation, we can no longer do without them. Also, it is often the only way to stay in touch with colleagues or people in countries where it is too dangerous to go. Also, don't forget that a lot of people consider them to be a mainstream medium. They'd rather read these than newspapers.

d For me, it is a way of staying in contact with my friends. But it's more than that because at work we use it as well and it helps me to keep informed about the projects my colleagues are involved in.

e I think it's absolutely cool. I add stuff to mine almost every day (that is, if my parents let me of course). I know a lot of them are uninteresting, but you know, you find the interesting ones soon enough.

B Do you keep, or have you ever kept, a diary? Why? Why not? What type of diary do you keep? Do you show it to others? How do you feel about someone reading your personal writing?

C Read the article about 'blogs'. The first sentence of each paragraph has been removed. As you read, try to find the right ones from the list on the next page. There is an extra sentence that you don't need.

Blog or die!

1 _____

Web logs (usually abbreviated to 'blogs') originated in the US in 1997 as a few online journals, often with links to news items on the World Wide Web plus brief, personal comments on those items by the writers ('bloggers'), as well as responses from readers. By mid-2002, the number of blogs had grown from only 23 at the start of 1999 to as many as 500,000 globally. Now there seem to be endless millions of them. This growth was fuelled by the spread of free blog-creation software, which removed the need for the blogger to be skilled in computer programming.

2 _____

The generally better quality of writing and the political stance of the blogger (often right-wing) distinguished these blogs from the more mundane online diaries. War bloggers included Andrew Sullivan, former editor of The Republican, whose blog reportedly received more than 800,000 visits in one month. Steve Reynolds, a University of Leicester law professor, drew around 43,000 visits in a single day to his blog site. Already in 2002 The Jerusalem Post reported that both Israeli and Palestinian bloggers were writing Web logs as a way to let the outside world see their sides of the ongoing Middle East conflict.

3 _____

Web logs' high site-visit figures made her and the mainstream media jumpy, especially as some of the new bloggers carried on their sites detailed criticism of stories in newspapers. A number of mainstream media outlets even added blogs to their websites, notably the British daily The Guardian, which ran a competition for the UK's best blog. The online magazine Slate incorporated an existing blog by Mike Paus, a former Newsview magazine reporter.

4 _____

Then, in 2002, the Web log came of age when the University of Chicago School of Journalism began offering a class on blogging, in which students created their own blogs. The course tutors were John Bitter, a co-founder of Info magazine, and Paul Saunders, programme director at the school.

5 _____

While veteran bloggers might object to the new, more politicised Web logs, blogging as a form of online communication is here to stay.

---

a John Thomas, a columnist at the Miami Globe, scathingly referred to blogs as an 'echo chamber of self-regard'.

b Web logs are not new, but as a forum for personal expression, they have sprouted prodigiously on the Internet, capturing new audiences, and have drawn significantly increased attention in the media.

c But just as the blog craze seemed to be taking off, Susan Freeman of the Newspapers' Association began voicing concerns.

d In the wake of the terrorist attacks in the US on 11 September 2001, a new type of Web log was born: the 'war blog'.

e In 2001, John Robb, president and chief operating officer of a blogging software developer, put forward a business use for Web logs, in which workers would use blogs as a medium to record and disseminate their thoughts.

f Blogging reached a huge, international audience following the US led invasion of Iraq, when millions followed the progress of the war courtesy of the Baghdad Blogger.

D Find words or phrases in the article that mean the following.

1 diaries

_____

2 grown

_____

3 writers

_____

4 helped

_____

5 everyday, usual

_____

6 nervous

_____

Reading

E Read the words. Without looking at the article, say what context they were used in.
Check your guess and then find a synonym or description.

1 abbreviated _____

2 responses _____

3 spread _____

4 distinguished _____

5 notably _____

6 came of age _____

7 scathingly _____

8 capturing _____

9 significantly _____

10 courtesy of _____

F What does the writer of the article mean by the following expressions?

1 … mainstream media …
_____

2 … politicised Web logs …
_____

3 … an echo chamber of self-regard …
_____

4 … sprouted prodigiously …
_____

5 … the blog craze seemed to be taking off …
_____

6 … to record and disseminate their thoughts …
_____

7 … in the wake of …
_____

G The Internet seems to be taking over from more traditional 'media' activities. We've read how Internet 'blogs' are taking over from writing ordinary diaries. Can you think of any other ways in which the Internet is taking over from more traditional ways of doing things?

Homework

Choose one of these two tasks.

1 Interview people (friends, relatives, colleagues) about modern communication methods (mobiles, blogs, chatrooms etc). Find out how they feel about them and if and how they use them.

2 Start a blog in which you track an important news event. Allow others to read it.

Listening and Speaking

A The following quotation is from a play written in 19th-century England. Do you think it's true? With a partner, discuss its meaning and implication.

'The pen is mightier than the sword.'

 B You are going to hear part of a daytime TV talk show. Read the statements below. Did the interviewee say these things? Tick (✓) the things that he says. The statements below are not direct quotes from the interview.

1   Censorship remains an important issue today.

2   The First Amendment to the US Constitution guarantees freedom of speech.

3   The First Amendment to the US Constitution guarantees freedom for newspapers.

4   The banned edition of *Little Red Riding Hood* encouraged people to drink alcohol.

5   A number of Shakespeare's plays were outlawed in schools in two American states.

6   Charles Darwin criticised the Bible.

7   The situation regarding the suppression of religious texts has deteriorated.

8   The Internet is banned in some countries.

9   Censorship is a sign of societal problems.

10 The world's great democracies trust their people.

 C Listen again. Which words in the interview mean the following?

a   of principal, central importance
_____

b   corrections
_____

c   unique, not happening repeatedly
_____

d   banned, removed
_____

e   different from the usual, not conventional
_____

f   says the opposite, disagrees with
_____

g   divided into opposing groups
_____

h   occurring locally, natural to an area
_____

i   self-satisfied
_____

j   the beginning, coming into being
_____

D Now use some of the above words to complete these sentences. You may need to change their form.

1 Don't be so _____! Check your answers!

2 The _____ population of Indonesia speaks over 300 different languages.

3 It's happened before. This is not an _____ incident.

4 Their positions are now so _____, I don't think they'll ever see eye-to-eye.

5 With the _____ of e-commerce, many shops have faced a tough time.

6 Just do what I say, and stop _____ me!

E You are going to hear five sentences. Each sentence contains an incorrect preposition. Write the correct preposition below.

■ EXAMPLE

You hear: He's sitting at the chair.

You write: on

---

1 _____

2 _____

3 _____

4 _____

5 _____

F Read Josh's blog entry on the role of the press. Discuss the questions.

1 How does this article relate to the topic of this unit?

2 Do you agree with this blogger? Explain.

3 List five facts and five opinions described in the article.

Entry for Monday 24 August: The role of the free press

Welcome to my blog where I comment on the news every day. I was so annoyed today!

The Army moved into yet another country on a humanitarian mission and again the press began covering the military action like a football game. Television programmes were interrupted so the viewers could be given an urgent special report. We watched the sliders land. We saw their hovercrafts. We saw their uniforms. We saw the starving people. And then we continued to watch the mission, one small step at a time, listening throughout to the news readers saying intelligent things just like sports commentators would do for any good sports game. Only in this case the news is out of place and undesirable. We enjoy a free press, however, we don't

need military shows. We want to know the facts and little else. We don't need to know about the number of bottles of water already used on the mission, and we don't need to have a twenty-four hour video line into the battle field.

We have let our press get out of control and it is time to stop. The key to ending this overkill is not to limit the right to a free press. The key is to let our news people know we are happy (or not) with the way they have chosen to use their freedom.

So, turn off your television when you feel the news is no longer news. Write or call the news directors at any network. Remember, the most important thing in news is ratings, and if it becomes clear that point will be lost, the big stations will quickly do something about it.

G Do you agree with the blogger? Why? Why not? You get to ask the UK Prime Minister or the United States president five questions about censorship, the media and the role of the government. With a partner, think of the five questions you would want to ask. Can you predict the answers?

Vocabulary and Writing

A Discuss the questions.

1 How many TV stations do you have in your country?

2 Do you have access to satellite TV in your country? Can you see programmes from other countries? If yes, which countries can you receive broadcasts from?

3 What other services are available for you via satellite?

B Read the following text quickly. Summarise its content. Who do you think this was written for? What publication would you find this in?

Watch it!

Your Satellite TV Watchdog

Welcome to July's round-up of satellite TV services in your area. Please remember we're always delighted to receive any feedback—your input helps keep us on our toes!

EuroTV

Well, the news from EuroTV this month comes as no surprise. Following the failure of takeover talks with ArtSA-TV and the resulting walkout by news staff after the crackdown on expense payments, a shake-up in personnel was inevitable. All a bit too late, though. The company will cease broadcasting on 1 August. Subscribers should contact their local office.

StarChannel

StarChannel, on the other hand, seems to go from strength to strength. Viewing figures suggest that the general downturn in new subscribers has not affected this broadcaster. The outlook remains good.

DV-TV

Despite the furore over some of the documentaries they have recently shown, the output from this station remains strong. Lower than average staff turnover has resulted in more consistency in programme quality. A breakthrough in technology is likely to result in improved pricing in the New Year. One to watch!

UK-Sat

Cutbacks in programme funding are starting to have an impact here. A very disappointing season so far and only likely to get worse.

ArtSA-TV

It was clear from the outset that ArtSA-TV, the stronger player, would never agree to EuroTV's demands. The drawbacks were immense. ArtSA-TV remains a solid performer with some of the least imaginative schedules. One to watch—but only if you're desperate!

C Find words in the text with the following meanings. You are looking for compound nouns and the first letter has been given. Check your answers with a partner.

1	summary	r
2	replies	f
3	contribution	i
4	the purchase of one company by another	t
5	strike	w
6	action against	c
7	change	s

8	decline	d
9	future prospect	o
10	production	o
11	change, replacement	t
12	important advance	b
13	reductions	c
14	start	o
15	negative aspects	d

D Here are some compound nouns based on phrasal verbs. Work with your partner and guess the meaning of the underlined word from its context.

1 Please fasten your seat belts and prepare for <u>take off</u>. _____

2 The media are claiming the Prime Minister ordered a <u>cover-up</u>. _____

3 Have you seen the headlines? 'OFFICIAL TAKES <u>KICKBACKS</u>.'
Apparently he got away with over $1 million dollars before he was caught. _____

4 The local newspaper has reported an increase in <u>break-ins</u> in the area. _____

5 The robbers made their <u>getaway</u> on a bicycle. That can't be right! _____

E Create some more compound nouns. In each of the following sentences, the preposition has been given, but not the verb. Choose an appropriate verb from the box. Check your answers with a partner.

print	turn	write	drop	hold	hand	check

1 There was an encouragingly large _____ out for the President's visit.

2 Did you see the news last night? There's been another _____ up at the bank in town.

3 Of course he doesn't have a good job. He was a high school _____ out at 15.

4 Could you get me a _____ out of the latest sales figures, please?

5 Please pay for your goods at the _____ -out.

6 Steve's lucky. He had so few injuries. The car was a _____ -off.

7 They distributed very few _____ outs at the conference.

F Work with your partner. Can you explain the difference between these pairs of compound nouns? Use a dictionary if necessary.

1 outlook / lookout

2 setup / upset

3 outlay / layout

4 uphold / holdup

5 outbreak / breakout

G Say what the underlined words in these headlines mean.

1 Government <u>axes</u> investment in education

2 <u>Bid</u> by South Africa for 2016 Olympics

3 Detectives <u>link</u> murder and explosions

4 FBI <u>pledge</u> to find killer

5 Woman's <u>ordeal</u> ends in disaster

H Newspaper headlines use few words, but try to make them as dramatic as possible. The aim is to catch the reader's eye. The following words often appear in newspaper headlines.

Headline words

aid	loom
axe	OK
back	ordeal
bid	oust
blast	pact
clash	plea
curb	pledge
cut	poll
drive	probe
go-ahead	talks
hike	threat
key	vow
link	wed

Meaning

help	likely to happen
cut, remove	approve, endorse
support	painful experience
attempt	push out, sack
explode, criticise	agreement
dispute	request
limit	promise
reduction	election, survey
campaign, effort	investigation
approval	discussions
increase, rise	danger
essential, vital	promise
connection	marry

I Look at the following newspaper headlines and explain what they mean in ordinary English.

1 Soap Star Weds Footie Star

_____

2 World Pledges Aid After Tsunami Disaster

_____

3 Managment In Bid To Curb Pay Hike

_____

4 US Airlines To Axe 1,000s Of Jobs

_____

5 Staff Blast Move To Oust Boss

_____

Language Practice

A Fill the gaps with 'in', 'on' or 'at'.

1 I read about this new 8 mega pixel _____ Camera Pix Magazine.

2 The CEO's office is _____ the 18th floor.

3 For Shanghai, you have to change planes _____ Hong Kong.

4 The news is _____ 9:00 pm.

5 It's not a good magazine. I read it _____ less than an hour.

6 John's having a sleepover _____ David's tonight.

7 If the plane's late, we won't get to Paris _____ time for supper.

8 Relax. I'll have dinner ready _____ five minutes.

B Choose the appropriate preposition to complete each sentence.

1 Budi came all the way_____ Malaysia for our wedding. (to / at / for)

2 She's so stuck up. She walked right _____ without a smile. (over / in / past)

3 How was I supposed to know he was standing _____ me? Do I have eyes in the back of my head? (next to / behind / beside)

4 His coat was so long it came way _____ his knees. (down / over / below)

5 The baby's ball rolled _____ the table onto the floor. (off / under / towards)

6 Use the ferry to get _____ the river; the bridge is dangerous. (on / across / past)

7 Please leave your boots _____ the door— they're filthy. (from / inside / by)

8 The box is _____ the wardrobe. Do you need the ladder? (on top of / below / over)

C 'Translate' the following newspaper headlines into everyday English.

1 PM Resigns. Gov't Turmoil Looms.

_____

_____

_____

2 City Centre Blast. Police Probe Terror Link.

_____

_____

_____

3 Poll: Fewer To Wed

_____

_____

_____

4 Gov't Pledge No Smoking Drive

_____

_____

_____

D Take the following five situations and write newspaper headlines for them. Remember, they should be as short as possible.

1   The government has approved a new drug for combatting AIDS.

_____

2   The police are about to begin an investigation into corruption in local government.

_____

3   An explosion in a discotheque has killed 200 people.

_____

4   A conference to establish peace in Sudan has failed.

_____

5   After the very hot summer, it is likely that water will be rationed soon.

_____

E Choose one of the headlines below and write about 50 words.

1   Man Eats Hamster
2   Bomb Blast Kills 200
3   Man Weds Dog In California
4   Language Learners Live Longer Probe Reveals

F Write a paragraph about some newsworthy events in your world, either from a personal point of view, or a regional, national or even international point of view. Use appropriate verb forms: the instructions will give you some hints.

1   Write about an event that happened in the recent past.
2   Write about an event that happened in the past but that still has effects on today.
3   Write about an event that was happening before something else happened.
4   Write about an event in the near future.
5   Write about an event that could happen, but may not.

Language Reference

PREPOSITIONS OF PLACE

in	inside	into	outside
on	on top of	onto	off
by	beside	next	to near
towards	to	from	among
under	above	below	in front of
up	down	behind	across
through	along	past	away from
round	around	opposite	between
out	of	at	over

'in' We use 'in' when something is surrounded on all sides, when we mean inside a building or when we refer to a town / street / country.

> He's in his room.
>
> I live in Cardiff.

'at' We use 'at' for a position, a point in space, to refer to a house / address or to refer to the normal use of a building.

> There's someone at the gate.
>
> He's sitting at his computer.
>
> He lives at 12 York Road.
>
> He's eating at the restaurant.

'on' We use 'on' for a surface or to refer to a floor somebody lives on.

> Can you put it on the tray, please?
>
> I live on the top floor.

PREPOSITIONS OF TIME

'in' We use 'in' to refer to a year / month / century, to refer to a longer period of time, or to refer to part of a day.

> My grandmother was born in 1940.
>
> We haven't got lessons in the summer term.
>
> I work best in the afternoon.

'In time' means early enough.

> He arrived in time for his flight.

'On time' means at the right time.

> His plane took off on time.

'at' We use 'at' to refer to clock time / meal time, to refer to a shorter period of time, or to refer to a day / date.

> I'll see you at 3 pm.
>
> I met him at the weekend.

'on' We use 'on' to refer to a day / date, to refer to a single day, or to refer to a part of a specific day.

> I saw him on Wednesday.
>
> Let's do something together on Christmas day.
>
> I'll phone you on Thursday morning.

HEADLINES

In headlines we often use compound nouns. They are often made of a verb + preposition.

Many compound nouns are based on phrasal verbs. Nouns formed from phrasal verbs often have an informal feel.

Notes:

1 Plurals are formed by adding 's' to the end or second part of the word.

> Kickbacks, break-ins.

2 Sometimes the phrasal verb is inverted to form the noun:

> to take over — takeover (verb + preposition)
>
> to turn down - downturn (preposition + verb)

3 Occasionally the noun is hyphenated:

> to break in — a break-in

4 The infinitive is used for future events.

> Man To Bite Dog (A man is going to bite a dog.)

5 Grammar words such as articles or auxiliary verbs are usually left out.

> Man Bites Dog (A man has bitten a dog.)

Medical matters

After this unit, you should be able to ...

- Discuss major diseases and health care systems
- Read about various medical conditions
- Use vocabulary related to medical conditions
- Recognise and use adverbial clauses
- Recognise and use subordinating conjunctions
- Write a health pamphlet

A What is the definition of the word 'disease'? How many different diseases can you name? Create a general list in groups and discuss them in class. Which diseases are considered the most serious? Which diseases are most common today?

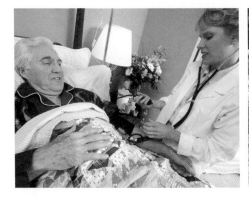

B Have you got any idioms or expressions in your language referring to medical matters? Remember that even though certain expressions contain medical references they don't always have to refer to a medical situation. Take a few minutes and write down any expressions you can think of and teach them to the class.

C Can you think of adverbs or adverb phrases that mean the same as 'and', 'but', 'because' and adverbs or adverb phrases that indicate a time sequence? Work with a partner and write down a list of your ideas. Compare with others and complete your list.

Listening

A What are some of the most serious medical problems people face in your country? Tick the diseases for your country. Compare your answers with others and complete the table for three other countries.

	my country	_____	_____	_____
heart disease				
breast cancer				
HIV / AIDS				
leukaemia				
stroke				
prostate cancer				
DVT (deep vein thrombosis)				
malnutrition				

B Listen to a news programme. Circle the biggest killer in the UK today.

a   beta-blockers   c   heart attacks   e   fatty diets

b   high cholesterol   d   heart disease

C What was actually said in the interview? Tick (✓) the statements that were made and cross (✗) the ones that were not.

1 ☐ We should worry about these developments.

2 ☐ There are many other, more important, problems.

3 ☐ Smoking makes it worse.

4 ☐ It's a disease that costs society a lot of money.

5 ☐ Insurance companies are not critical enough.

6 ☐ We needed to find out whether hospitals were using their money well.

7 ☐ Many people suffering from heart disease are going to be afraid.

8 ☐ People were not helped quickly enough.

9 ☐ Staff running hospitals are not as competent as we think.

10 ☐ Sometimes people go to hospital too late.

11 ☐ Eating too much fat is an important factor contributing to heart disease.

12 ☐ Physical exercise is a must for people in our society.

13 ☐ Beta-blockers make it easier for the heart to work.

14 ☐ People don't have to take the medicine.

15 ☐ This was the first time hospitals were under scrutiny.

16 ☐ The results of the experiments were astonishing.

D Are these statements are true or False? Listen again to check your answers.

1 **T F** Dr Moore is a cardiologist from the Royal College of Physicians.
2 **T F** The Royal College of Physicians set two targets to monitor hospital performance.
3 **T F** The study was conducted over a two-year period.
4 **T F** Most hospitals were able to hit the first target successfully.
5 **T F** Many people mistake heart attack symptoms for something else and thus delay getting themselves to the Emergency Room.
6 **T F** The first treatment for a heart attack victim is an injection of statins.
7 **T F** The first target was not an easy target to hit.
8 **T F** Beta-blockers are drugs used to control high cholesterol.
9 **T F** More than half of hospitals hit the second target.
10 **T F** Dr Moore thinks that the results are very discouraging.

E Match the words from the audio to the definitions.

1	physicians			a	find out
2	exacerbated			b	ways of doing something
3	ascertain			c	given to you by a doctor
4	resources			d	doctors
5	potential			e	high blood pressure
6	symptoms			f	possible
7	diagnosis			g	made worse
8	hypertension			h	things you are able to use
9	prescribed			i	effects of an illness
10	strategies			j	identification of a disease

F What could be done by hospitals to improve their performance in the areas described in the radio programme? Fill the table with your ideas.

Financing	Response time	Public Information	Follow-up programmes

G What do you think are the major problems faced by hospitals today? Why?

A Read the article about HIV / AIDS. Underline any vocabulary that is unfamiliar to you.
Test a fellow student on these words and phrases.

Awareness

Today, HIV / AIDS is considered to be the one of the most lethal and terminal diseases in history. Having claimed the lives of over 25 million people since 1981, there is no known cure for this devastating disease. Doctors and researchers all over the world work tirelessly to discover a cure but have so far only been somewhat successful in establishing a treatment to slow down the mortality and morbidity rates of HIV. According to the World Health Organisation (WHO), there are currently 38.6 million people living with this disease.

Originally termed 'Gay-Related Immune Deficiency' (GRID), it was quickly determined that HIV / AIDS was not a homosexual disease. In 1982, the Centre for Disease Control (CDC) changed the acronym to AIDS, Acquired Immune Deficiency Syndrome, as there were more heterosexual patients than homosexual ones. Both men and women are susceptible to contracting the disease as well as children. Transference can occur through the passing of a bodily fluid of one person into the bloodstream of another. Sex is the most common form of transference, however blood transfusions, sharing of hypodermic needles and even breast milk are also ways to pass the disease on to others.

The origin of HIV / AIDS has been traced back to the Congo region in Africa. One theory is that researchers working on a cure for polio inadvertently opened the door to releasing the HIV virus. However, this theory has been refuted by some in the medical community and has not been validated. Basically, the HIV virus has been determined as coming from the common chimpanzee. How the virus was transferred from primate to human

is still a mystery but there are now two strains of HIV (Human Immunodeficiency Virus) that currently exist. HIV-1 is the most common form. HIV-2 is not as readily spread but is a serious medical matter in West African regions.

While most people are now aware of and have been educated about HIV / AIDS, there is still some confusion as to what having this disease means. In actuality, HIV is not the same as AIDS. The two are definitely joined together in a morbid marriage. However, people often feel that if a person has been diagnosed with HIV this means they have AIDS too. This is not true. HIV is the actual virus that manifests itself within the blood cells of a host. It is a 'retroviral' virus meaning a person can live with HIV but not develop AIDS. Currently, once doctors detect the HIV virus in a patient, they can administer a treatment known as 'antiretroviral', which delays the development of AIDS but cannot cure the effects the virus has on the human body. HIV can have a gestation period of nine to ten years even without the antiretroviral treatment. AIDS occurs when a patient's immune system has been degraded by the HIV virus and can no longer fight off even the simplest of infections. At this point, even a common cold can be fatal to an AIDS patient. Once AIDS has presented itself in a patient, the estimated life expectancy is around nine months.

As this disease has taken hold of millions of people and claimed the lives of many more, the research for a cure for AIDS has become the focus of many charitable events hosted by famous celebrities to raise funds for continued efforts to eradicate this devastating disease. Numerous clinics, hospices and hospitals have adapted themselves to accommodate people living with AIDS and 1 December has been named World AIDS Awareness Day. The red ribbon has also become synonymous with the fight against AIDS and is one of the most recognisable symbols around the world.

B Match these words from the article to the meanings. Try not to use a dictionary but to work them out from the context.

1	lethal	☐	☐	a	the time period it takes for something to develop
2	tirelessly	☐	☐	b	to work with determination and concentration
3	mortality	☐	☐	c	a word formed from the initials of other words
4	morbidity	☐	☐	d	loss of life on a large scale
5	acronym	☐	☐	e	accessible or sensitive to something
6	susceptible	☐	☐	f	the effect of one object on another unintentionally
7	transference	☐	☐	g	causing death
8	hypodermic	☐	☐	h	unwholesome, melancholy, related to disease
9	inadvertently	☐	☐	i	the breed or group of a virus
10	strain	☐	☐	j	the action of moving one object to another space
11	manifest	☐	☐	k	to make clear to the eye or in understanding something
12	gestation	☐	☐	l	the introduction of medicine or drugs under the skin

C Read the text again and answer the questions True or False.

1 **T F** AIDS only affects on section of the community?

2 **T F** Scientists have given up trying to find a cure for AIDS.

3 **T F** Some people believe that AIDS is a man-made disease.

4 **T F** HIV is another name for AIDS.

5 **T F** HIV-2 is more localised than HIV-1.

6 **T F** HIV can be cured.

7 **T F** Someone might have HIV for ten years and not know.

8 **T F** World AIDS Day was set up to celebrate a breakthrough in the fight against AIDS.

D Look at the list of conditions. Make sure you understand what each disease or condition is. What do you know about these diseases or medical conditions?

1	cancer	5	eczema
2	Alzheimer's	6	dementia
3	emphysema	7	malnutrition
4	athlete's foot	8	schizophrenia

E Allergies are very common and a rather large percentage of people suffer from them. Discuss the questions. Take notes.

1 Do you suffer from allergies? Or know someone who does?

2 If yes, what are you allergic too?

3 Can allergies be life threatening?

4 What are some common allergies people have?

5 What are some of environmental factors that cause allergies?

6 There have been reports that today more children suffer from allergies than ever before. Why do think this might be?

7 What could people do to prevent allergies?

Homework

Using your notes answers from Exercise E, write a one-page essay about allergies. Include all the topics, their main points and use the new vocabulary introduced. Summarize your points and form into paragraphs – introduction, body and conclusion. Bring your essay to the next class for peer review and class display.

Vocabulary

A Look at the idioms below. They are related to medical matters but are not always used in a medical context. What do you think they mean?

1   look like death warmed up
_____

2   be back on one's feet
_____

3   break out
_____
_____

4   on the mend
_____
_____

5   go under the knife
_____

6   have a taste of one's own medicine
_____
_____

7   have a clean bill of health
_____

8   a bitter pill to swallow
_____

9   be as sick as a dog
_____

10 hack up a lung
_____

B Complete the sentences with the correct idiom from Exercise A.

1   Next Thursday my aunt has to _____
    She's really nervous about it.

2   Well Mr. Smith, I'd say you have a
    _____ Congratulations!

3   I couldn't go into work today as was as
    _____.

4   'How's your mother doing?' 'Oh she's
    _____. She'll be fine soon'.

5   'Gosh, that cough really sounds bad.' 'I know.
    I feel like I'm going to _____.'

6   After the last stock market crash it took the
    company a while to get _____.

7   He's such an idiot! I'd love to give him a
    _____.

8   'You look terrible!' 'Yeah, I _____
    _____.'

C As a class, think of real world situations where the above idioms would be used in conversation. Remember they do not have to necessarily refer to medical conditions. In small groups, create a conversation using at least five of the idioms in context. Present your conversations to the class.

D Write definitions for the words on the list below. If you aren't sure, look up the words in an English / English dictionary.

1   calluses _____

2   ingrown (nail) _____

3   bunions _____

4   deformities _____

5   warts _____

6   skin graft _____

7   administer _____

8   tumour _____

E Below is a list of types of doctors specialising in different areas of medicine. Match the type of doctor to their job description.

allergist	cardiologist
occupational therapist	ophthalmologist
physiotherapist	podiatrist
orthopaedic surgeon	dermatologist

1 _____ : treats calluses, ingrown toenails, corns, bunions, ankle and foot injuries. They often prescribe medicine, physical therapy and do surgery if required. They also create and fit special objects to help correct deformities. Sometimes they make custom-made shoes.

2 _____ : treats skin problems such as acne, hives, rashes and warts often with lotions and prescription medications. They are also skin surgeons, sometimes performing skin grafts and helping to prevent certain skin diseases. They treat patients of all ages.

3 _____ : examines and tests for heart diseases and treats heart attack victims. They do not perform surgery but can administer ECGs (echocardiogrammes). They must have an excellent understanding of biology, chemistry, health and psychology.

4 _____ : deals with the assessment and treatment of the bones, muscles and connecting tissues. They treat patients of all ages from infants to adults and most often people who play sports or have been in an accident. They can perform surgery to replace joints and repair broken bones with metal pins or plastic mouldings.

5 _____ : rehabilitates people who need help to improve, develop or keep practical skills. They often work with people in wheelchairs, who have lost a limb, have had a back injury, etc, and need to re-learn how to use or adjust their bodies to doing everyday activities.

6 _____ : studies and treats eye disorders. They perform eye exams, prescribe eyeglasses, treat eye diseases and perform eye surgery. Through their examinations they can often detect high blood pressure, diabetes and brain tumours.

7 _____ : helps patients with disabilities, diseases or injury. Their services are often prescribed by other doctors in order to help people recover physically from their ailments. They tend to use many different forms of treatment depending on the type of disability.

F Imagine you work in a hospital and you are showing a group of students around. Without referring back to Exercise E, tell your partner what each of these doctors does. Write short descriptions but use your own words.

---EXAMPLE---------------------

This is Dr Brown. She is a ... She ...

----

1 podiatrist

2 dermatologist

3 cardiologist

4 orthopaedic surgeon

5 occupational therapist

6 ophthalmologist

7 physiotherapist

G Circle the word that doesn't belong. What is the relationship between the other three words?

1 a surgery   c anaesthesia
   b operation   d procedure

2 a doctor   c care-giver
   b physician   d podiatrist

3 a rash   c acne
   b blood   d warts

4 a diagnosis   c establish
   b assessment   d prognosis

5 a illness   c ailment
   b sickness   d podiatrist

6 a medicine   c treatment
   b hypodermic needle d shots

7 a cot   c bed
   b stretcher   d trolley

8 a doctor's office c clinic
   b nurse   d dentist's office

9 a stethoscope   c forceps
   b scalpel   d bone

10 a ECG   c x-ray
   b echocardiogramme d blood donation

Grammar and Vocabulary

A Subordinating conjunctions are used to create adverbial clauses. Listen to the passage and underline the adverbial clauses that will help.

1 _____
_____, it is probable
that one in twenty-seven will die from it.

2 ... many groups and organisations hold annual
events, such as the CIBC Run for the Cure in
Canada, _____
_____
_____.

3 _____,
breast cancer has come to the foreground over the
last few years.

4 _____
_____, it is becoming more common in
males.

5 There is no finite age group targeted for this disease
_____.

6 Women aged fifty and older should also get a
mammogram every 2 years that will help _____
_____
_____.

7 Many doctors are also teaching their patients how to
administer self-examinations _____
_____
_____.

8 Family history also plays a part _____
_____
_____
_____.

9 _____, a doctor must determine the
status of the lump.

10 _____, education and awareness of breast
cancer will continue to be the leading form of prevention.

B Identify the type of adverbial clause in the sentences in Exercise A. Tick the correct boxes.

	contrast	purpose	time	degree	condition	cause
1						
2						
3						
4						
5						
6						
7						
8						
9						
10						

C What is the purpose of the conjunctions below. Check your answers with another classmate.

if	whether	because	after	to the extent that
when	as long as	since	once	in so far as
even	though	as	until	so that
if	although	when	where	in order that
unless	even though	whenever	wherever	that
provided that	as if	while	in	
assuming that	while	before	as much as	

1 to show condition
2 to show contrast
3 to show cause
4 to show time
5 to show place
6 to show degree
7 to show purpose

D Write sentences using the vocabulary provided. You will need to add subordinating conjunctions to complete the sentences. Don't forget to capitalise the first letter of your sentence and to use punctuation at the end!

1 can / look at your throat / to open / he / your mouth / the doctor / will ask / you

_____

_____

2 twice a day / need to / take these tablets / you / you have eaten.

_____

_____

3 course of antibiotics / symptoms / continue / the entire / clear up / your / to take

_____

_____

4 sit / come in / please / and / you like / as long

_____

_____

5 John's mother / him / to teach / she / knew / took / to the doctor / him / a lesson / he wasn't really ill

_____

_____

6 ring / a slight cold / you / can't / you / have / the doctor /

_____

_____

7 what is wrong / go to / with you / don't / you / you / will never / the doctor / know /

_____

_____

8 a / was training / had to work / hours / she / Karen / to be / doctor / very long

_____

_____

9 should always / serious / you / visit / have / a doctor / chest pains / it / you / could be

_____

_____

10 quietly / should / you / have / you / and take / a headache / sit / an aspirin

_____

_____

E Study the afflictions people can experience. What type of medical practitioner would you consult for these?

1	a rash	_____
2	an irregular heartbeat	_____
3	a blister	_____
4	a headache	_____
5	stomach pains	_____
6	back pain	_____
7	dry skin	_____
8	an irritated eye	_____
9	an infected wound	_____
10	pain in your knee or wrist joints	_____
11	foot injury	_____
12	back injury after an accident	_____

a podiatrist   e occupational therapist

b dermatologist   f ophthalmologist

c cardiologist   g physical therapist

d orthopaedist   h GP

F If you were in need of seeing a specialist, how would you describe your symptoms? Work with a partner. Look at the list of adjectives and decide which ones can be used to describe the symptoms below. Some adjectives can be used for more than one ailment.

recurring	pounding	throbbing	unbearable
excruciating	scratchy	itchy	tender
sharp	watery	weeping	thumping
flaky	dull	severe	nauseating
cutting	razor-sharp	crippling	stiff

a rash	an irregular heartbeat
a blister	a headache
stomach pains	back pain
dry skin	an irritated eye
an infected wound	pain in your knee or wrist joints

Reading and Vocabulary

A Answer these questions with a partner from a different country. Tell the class what you have learned about health care in your partner's country.

1 Is health care free in your country or do you have to pay?

2 If you have to pay, is it subsidised?

3 If it is free, how is it paid for?

4 What exactly (if anything) do you have to pay for?

5 Is it expensive?

6 What problems are caused by your health care being free / having to pay for it?

B Match the words to the definitions.

1 series of articles ☐	☐ a	something that is extraordinary or remarkable
2 national disgrace ☐	☐ b	the beginning
3 charging ☐	☐ c	applying a cost or fee to something
4 restructuring of a society ☐	☐ d	to bring shame or discredit a country
5 aim ☐	☐ e	minimal; not a huge amount
6 outset ☐	☐ f	to cause stress or anxiety to a person
7 phenomenal ☐	☐ g	a group of writings based on one topic
8 inception ☐	☐ h	the start or the beginning of something, such as an idea
9 nominal ☐	☐ i	to make a choice
10 innovation ☐	☐ j	improving or changing an environment to become better
11 to be a strain ☐	☐ k	a new creation
12 to opt for (something) ☐	☐ l	a goal or final result

C Read the article about the British National Health Service. Underline any words or phrases you do not know and talk about their meaning with fellow students.

Health Care around the World: The NHS

With health care an increasingly big issue, we continue our series of articles looking at health systems in other countries. This week, we look at the British National Health Service (NHS).

Health care in pre-1950s Britain was a bit of a national disgrace. Although it was one of the richest and most powerful countries on earth, all but the poorest people had to pay for medical services, which meant that many could not afford to visit a doctor in any but the most extreme circumstances. From the middle of the nineteenth century, people began to accept the need for free health care. A few attempts were made to open charitable institutions which would provide free health care, most notably the Royal Free Hospital in London. However, all of these institutions had to start charging in the end.

As part of the restructuring of British society following the Second World War, the UK government decided, in 1948, to establish the National Health Service, the aim of which was to provide high-quality free health care for all. Costs would be met via taxation. From the very outset, the costs of the NHS were phenomenal and, only three years after its inception, small fees were introduced for prescribed drugs. However, these were charged at a nominal rate of one shilling (approximately 10 cents), which was heavily subsidised.

The main innovation of the NHS was to set up a network of family doctors or general practitioners (GPs) who were based in surgeries within the community. These doctors would treat patients where appropriate and would refer more serious cases to the hospitals. In this way, they were able to take the pressure off the hospitals, which only had to deal with emergencies and more serious cases. Also established at this time were community health centres, which were responsible for preventative medicine on a local level. The GPs, health centres and hospitals were administered by local health authorities.

The NHS has served the British public well over the last five or six decades. Although costs have always been a strain on the public purse and more charges, particularly for dental care, have been introduced, access to health care is still on the whole free for all Britons. The main issues today are those of waiting lists which determine how long a patient has to wait before receiving a hospital appointment after being referred by a GP. Recent extensions in funding and innovations in hospital funding have gone some way to addressing this.

Whatever the future for the NHS, as an experiment in providing high-quality free or affordable health care for all, it has been quite successful and only time will tell if the British people continue to opt for this kind of arrangement.

D Read the text once more. Find words that mean the same as the vocabulary below.

1　magazine features

_____

2　actions people provide

_____

3　not requiring payment

_____

4　set up

_____

5　importantly

_____

6　note from doctor allocating drugs

_____

7　tackling an issue

_____

8　choose

_____

E Make a list of the words you underlined from the reading. Work in small groups and compare your lists. Ask your partners in your groups if they know the meaning of the words you underlined. Do not use your dictionaries. If no one in the group knows the meaning, ask your teacher.

F In groups, compare the health care systems of Britain and your country. Note any similarities or differences between the two.

Homework　Using the information from Exercise F, write a comparison between the two health care systems. Use adverbs and adverb phrases you learned earlier in this unit and the vocabulary you have studied from the article. Your writing should be about four to five paragraphs. In class, exchange your writing with a fellow student and do peer review.

A Use the following points and write an instructional paragraph on how a doctor would assess a patient. What would the doctor do first, second, third, etc.?

EXAMPLE

When a patient goes to see a doctor, there is a certain procedure the doctor uses to assess the patient's problems. First ...

ask the patient to identify symptoms

treat and correct the condition

examine the patient

follow up appointment

recommend tests and blood work

B These sentences contain some of the most common errors made by students of English. Read the sentences and underline the errors and re-write the sentences correctly.

1   Laughter is often called the better medicine.
_____
_____

2   Janice ranged the hospital to enquire for her son's condition.
_____
_____

3   The doctors took a good care of me when I was in a hospital.
_____
_____

4   I am sorry to hear you can come to my party. We must get together when you are feeling more better.
_____
_____

5   You should be careful! You almost took the wrong pills by error.
_____
_____

6   I am really disinterested in hearing about other people's illnesses. It's so boring!
_____
_____

7   New drug-resistant viruses are menacing world health.
_____
_____

8   Congratulations! I heard you have past your medical exams.
_____
_____

9   It can't be chicken-pox. I had already had that as a child.
_____
_____

10   Dear Mr Brown, Thanks a lot for your letter of 25th March ...
_____
_____

C Listen to a dictation. Write down key words and phrases. Do not worry about correct spelling as you write. This will be addressed after the dictation is finished.

1   _____

2   _____

3   _____

4   _____

5   _____

6   _____

7   _____

8   _____

9   _____

10   _____

D Most of the time you can get the main ideas of a written text from key vocabulary. Study some of the key vocabulary from the audio. Review the notes you took and write a definition for each of these terms based on how they were used in context. Do not use a dictionary.

1 distorted body image

_____

_____

2 conquer one's appetite

_____

_____

3 hunger pains

_____

_____

4 despite the fact (that)

_____

_____

5 binges

_____

_____

6 get rid of

_____

_____

7 laxatives

_____

_____

8 tend to occur

_____

_____

9 life threatening

_____

_____

10 detected and treated

_____

_____

E Learning to correct your own mistakes in writing is a very important skill. The process is rather similar to the paragraph you wrote in Exercise A. Fill the missing verbs for each of these stages.

Stage 1: _____ the text

Stage 2: _____ errors

Stage 3: _____ corrections

Stage 4: _____ the text

F In small groups, consider what would be common grammar mistakes to search for in your writing. Make a list of your ideas then compare with the class.

G Exchange your dictation from Exercise D with a partner. Check your partner's writing for spelling and grammar mistakes but do not correct it! Just circle or underline any errors you find. If you are not sure, confer with another student or your teacher. Return the writing to your partner. Now, look at the errors indicated in your own writing and make corrections.

H Use the notes from the dictation to write a 200-word article about anorexia and bulimia. Use your own words to combine ideas. Use linking-words and adverbial phrases.

Homework   Rewrite your article into a final draft and hand it in to your teacher for final corrections.

Language Practice

A Fill the gaps with an appropriate idiom.

back on your feet	as sick as a dog	a clean bill of health
a bitter pill to swallow	a taste of his own medicine	feel like death warmed up
on the mend	go under the knife	

1 I will get my revenge on him! He's going to get _____.

2 I can't stop sneezing, I have a sore throat, a headache and I have to blow my nose every five minutes! I _____

3 Go to bed and take three aspirin. You will be _____ in no time.

4 There's nothing wrong with you! The doctor gave you _____, so stop moaning and get out of bed!

5 Some medicines can taste terrible or have severe side-effects therefore they can literally be _____.

6 'How's Kirsten?' 'She just found out she has to _____ next week!'

7 Get some rest and don't worry about anything. You'll be _____ in no time.

8 'Are you better?' 'No, actually, I'm _____. It's hopeless!'

B Match the words to their uses.

'if' 'though' 'as' 'whenever'	a to show condition
'because' 'when' 'while'	b to show contrast
'where' 'even if' 'in so far as'	
'to the extent that'	c to show cause
'unless' 'in as much as'	
'provided that' 'since'	
'although' 'in order that'	d to show time
'assuming that' 'since'	
'whether' 'after that'	e to show place
'as long as' 'wherever'	
'as if' 'once' 'so that'	f to show degree
'before' 'until' 'even though'	
'when' 'while'	g to show purpose

C Complete the gaps with an appropriate subordinating conjunction.

1 _____ you feel better, continue to take the pills.

2 Please get on the table, _____ I can take an X-ray.

3 _____ you feel tired, sit down and take a rest.

4 Your cholesterol is very high _____ you eat too many fatty foods.

5 _____ you stop smoking, the problem will go away.

6 James was sent to the ICU, _____ he could receive round-the-clock care.

7 _____ you have your anaesthetic, a nurse will give you a pre-med.

8 He was admitted to hospital overnight to be on the safe side _____ it appeared that he was OK.

9 Please take a seat, _____ I need to ask you a few questions.

10 _____ I have seen your X-rays, I will be able to make a diagnosis.

D Form sentences from the fragments and use the subordinating conjunction in the brackets.
Pay attention to verb / subject agreements and verb tenses and punctuation.

1 wake up / arrive / to work / Ken / late / on time / he (even though)
<u>Even though Ken woke up late, he arrived to work</u>
<u>on time.</u>

2 has / she / a secret / is / act / she (as if) _____
_____

3 the concert / can / homework / you / do / go / your / to (provided that) _____
_____

4 stop / saw / documentary / on / I / smoking / lung disease / I / that (since) _____
_____

5 cold / I / always / weather / get / a / change (whenever) _____
_____

6 education / HIV / AIDS / best / cure / they / a / find / prevention / for / the / is (until) _____
_____

7 breast cancer / be / your / sometimes / can / hereditary / history / in / it / family / is (assuming that)
_____
_____

8 not / NHS / successful / future / it / be / certain / work / the / continue / to / is / will / in (whether) _____
_____

9 research / heart disease / be / people / do / die / expected / on / to / be (before) _____
_____

10 need / can / medication / take / schizophrenics / society / in / function / to / they (so that) _____
_____

E Read the passage and underline the errors.

There are much disease on the world today. Cancer, heart disease, mentel illness, blood disorders and many more are all causes of concern for many people. Governments tried to help by allocating a largest amount of funds to health care so that the general public can have access to doctors in places such as Britain and South Africa. Privatized health care is becomed more popular while only wealthier people can afford it. A lot of research is been done to find cures for many of these diseases and some did be successful but there is still a long way to go.

Education can be one of the best preventions doctors and health officials can provide. If the public knew how to assess and recognise the symptoms of certain disease, they will be able to detection of an illness early and be treated. Eating the healthier diet, doing regular exercise, quitting smoking and getting lots of sleep as well, aid in the fight against disease. Even, you don't suffer from a sickness, you might know someone who does it. Understanding, patience and support can truly help at a person's recovery. Hopefully, one day, health care will be free for everyone and the world would be a happier, healthier place.

Language Reference

ADVERBIAL CLAUSES

An adverbial clause is a group of words with a verb, starting with a conjunction, which modifies the main verb or the main clause in the sentence.

If you don't feel well, you can make an appointment to see Dr Jones.

Make an appointment to see the nurse, provided that you don't feel any better.

Adverbial clauses can go before or after the main clause in the sentence. They are introduced by a subordinate conjunction. They can be used to show condition, contrast, cause, time, place, degree and purpose.

The basic form of an adverbial clause at the beginning of a sentence is:

subordinate conjunction + subject + verb + main clause

If you take these pills, you will feel better.

The basic form of an adverbial clause at the end of a sentence is:

main clause + subordinate conjunction + subject + verb

You will feel better if you take these pills.

CONJUNCTIONS

Conjunctions: 'if', 'when', 'even if', 'unless', 'provided that', 'assuming that', 'whether', 'as long as'

Purpose: to show condition

Unless you take out a health insurance policy, your family will receive nothing when you die.

Conjunctions: 'though', 'although', 'even though', 'as if', 'while'

Purpose: to show contrast

Even though he had never been sick all his life, he regularly had a medical check-up.

Conjunctions: 'because', 'since', 'as'

Purpose: to show cause

I knew that something was wrong, because he had been complaining about pain in his chest for weeks.

Conjunctions: 'when', 'whenever', 'while', 'as', 'before', 'after', 'since', 'once', 'until'

Purpose: to show time

Once he had had the operation, he was as fit as a fiddle.

Conjunctions: 'where', 'wherever'

Purpose: to show place

Wherever he went, he could never get a satisfactory explanation for the disease.

Conjunctions: 'in as much as', 'to the extent that', 'in so far as'

Purpose: to show degree

In as much as the doctor told her, she knew there was something terribly wrong.

Conjunctions: 'so that', 'in order that', 'that'

Purpose: to show purpose

I decided to consult an occupational therapist, so that I'd feel better.

COMMON VERBS USED TO DESCRIBE ILLNESSES

All of these verbs are used to say how a person is feeling:

I have a headache and pain behind my eyes.

I'm very nauseous first thing in the morning.

Tom experiences a sharp pain in his foot every time he goes running.

My mother suffers from chronic arthritis.

She gets an irregular heartbeat if she exercises too hard.

Risky business!

After this unit, you should be able to ...

- Listen to an expert speak about risk-taking
- Take notes on risk-taking behaviour
- Read about setting up your own business
- Use conjunctions accurately
- Listen about extreme sports
- Encourage someone to and discourage someone from taking an action
- Write a leaflet

A Think about a risk that you have taken in your life. It might be physical risk, or a social risk, or a financial risk or something else. Discuss these questions and take notes.

1 What was the risk that you took?

2 What were the potential gains to taking the risk?

3 What were the potential losses to taking the risk?

4 How did you feel just before you took the risk? And after?

5 What was the outcome?

6 Can you put your finger on why you took the risk?

7 Would you do it again?

B Security is a fundamental human need. In the light of this, how can we explain risk-taking behaviour? Why do people take risks? Discuss with a partner and share your explanation with the class.

Listening and Speaking

A Do you often think about why people behave the way they do, or is human behaviour a mystery to you? With a partner, make a short list of motivational factors for human behaviour: what makes people behave the way they do?

B You are going to listen to a radio broadcast. Try to put the headings in the order that the speaker mentions them. Write your answers in the space provided.

_____ Categories of Risk-Taking Behaviour

_____ Categories of Risk-Takers

_____ Risk Taking and Evolution

_____ What is a Risk

_____ What Accounts for Differences in Risk-Taking Behaviour?

C You will now hear the interview again. Take notes about each of the headings. As you take notes, do not try to write complete sentences. Write down key words and phrases. When the interview is finished, take some time to fill in your notes with any information that is still fresh in your memory.

D Use your notes and memory to complete the summary.

Professor Robert Wilson defined a risk as the probability that some (1) _____ event will happen, usually as the result of our behaviour. He said that in recent years, people's interest in engaging in dangerous activities, such as extreme sports, has been (2) _____, and although experts have shown us that some of the habits we once thought harmless, such as (3) _____, are actually quite harmful, people (4) _____ to do them. Risk-taking behaviour is part of what has made humans such a (5) _____ species. Professor Wilson accounted for individual differences in the willingness to take risks by describing a personality continuum. At one end, we have (6) _____, who are generally known to play it safe. Then there are those who have their limits, weighing up the risk against the gain. These people are known as (7) _____ Finally there are the risk optimisers, who are attracted to taking risks. Recent studies have also divided risks themselves into four categories. The first is referred to as 'thrill seeking'. This trait is associated with taking (8) _____ risks. A second category is 'experience seeking', gaining new experiences from risks, and is associated with (9) _____ behaviour. The third category is '(10) _____'. This is associated with what could be called (11) _____ risks, like drinking, smoking or drug taking. The final category is the 'boredom threshold'. Some people get bored more easily than others and will take risks to (12) _____ their boredom.

E Read these statements and using your notes from Exercise C, identify what category of risks the following people describe.

1 I just want to get the most out of life. Sometimes my friends try to discourage me from the things I do. They can't imagine why I would do such risky things. I just want to know everything about the world that I can. To do that, I need to get a good sense of where the boundaries lie. I just don't think you are really living if you can always predict a secure outcome for everything you do. Shake it up a bit!
Adrian— 25, USA

2 'Extreme sports are just wicked, man! There is nothing like the adrenaline rush you get from them ...'
Charlotte— 19, Australia

3 'Yes, I smoke, drink and eat fast food. I would rather enjoy myself than go through life miserably.'
Matthew — 47, UK

4 'My job is so tedious that I just have to get some excitement at weekends. That's why I go snowboarding.'
Phil — 32, Sweden

F Construct a questionnaire to find out what kind of personality your classmates have when it comes to risk taking. You can ask people about their experiences, their attitudes, or how they would react in a hypothetical situation. Be sure that anticipated answers will shed light on which category your classmates fall into. When you have finished poll all of the students in the class. Don't forget to ask your teacher!

G Rejoin your partner and analyse the results of your survey. Create a bar graph on an overhead transparency or a piece of chart paper. Briefly present your results to the class. Since everyone in the class surveyed the same group, the results should be very similar. Are they?

Homework

Imagine that you are an outdoor activities company. Create a full-page advertisement advertising your services. Your advertisement should be geared to one kind of risk-taking behaviour. Make sure that your activities, encouragement and language would appeal to your target market.

Reading

A Read the article. What did Antonia do and has she been successful?

Out on her Own

Every year, thousands of people in this country quit their jobs and start their own businesses. Although many small businesses fail and only a lucky few end up becoming self-made millionaires, for the majority of those willing to take the risk, it can be very rewarding indeed. Here Joanna Moss talks to Antonia Bacon, who set up her own knitting business a few years ago.

1

'Well, I had spent ten years working as a lawyer in a large city practice and really felt that I wasn't going anywhere. Yes, I was quite successful and had had some good promotions, but really my heart wasn't in it any more. I was working from eight in the morning to sometimes as late as ten at night when we were preparing a case, and I felt that this had become my life. Even at weekends, I was too tired to enjoy myself with my family or to have any hobbies.'

2

'Well, I have always knitted since I was quite young. In fact, you might say that I come from a family of knitters. My mother and my grandmother were always knitting around the house, and I learnt the craft from them. Well, due to my work, I hadn't had time to do any knitting for a few years but have got loads of hand-knitted garments which I either made in my youth or got from my mother. My friends used to remark on how much they liked them and ask where they could get them, and I had to tell them that they were one-offs. My grandmother had a natural eye for colour and used to knit the most wonderful patterns that she invented. Well, one day, I agreed to try and recreate one for a friend during my holidays, and she was so delighted with the outcome that she told all her friends, and they wanted them too. Well, I couldn't make any more as I had no time but had really enjoyed making the one for my friend. One evening at dinner, my husband, who could tell I hadn't been happy for a while, suggested that I give up work and take up knitting full-time.'

3

'Well, not really. Although I knew there was a demand, I was worried that orders might not materialise or people might not be prepared to pay a fair price for my hand knits. So, I sat down and worked out a proper business plan. This is a must for anyone thinking of setting up their own business. I sat down and worked out how much I would need to spend on raw materials, how many sweaters I could produce per month, and how much I could charge per sweater. I also approached quite a few local boutiques to see if any of them would buy my sweaters to sell in their shops.'

4

'Well, firstly I had realistic expectations. I wanted to be able to make enough money to pay myself a reasonable monthly salary and to be able to reinvest in raw materials. I didn't expect that this would make me rich, but wanted to be sure that a reasonable number of working hours per week would support me in a lifestyle that I wanted.'

5

'Well, I wasn't sure, and knew that I was taking a big risk. But, as I had set myself reasonable expectations, I felt that things would work out. Something at the back of my mind was saying 'Hey, if it was that easy, everybody would be setting up their own businesses,' but I think that the reason people don't is that they are scared to take the risk. For the majority of those who do take the risk, things work out, and if things didn't work out for me, at least I would have tried.'

6

'No, not at all. I am finally doing something that I really enjoy. I am working from home, which has many advantages, particularly with regard to seeing my children, and what's more, I am my own boss. If I want to take an afternoon off for a special event, I can. I can fix my own working hours and take on as much or as little work as I feel I want or need to.'

7

'Go for it, but be very careful in working out your business plan and set yourself reasonable goals. You are not going to get rich quickly, but as long as you are making enough to keep yourself comfortable, the payoffs are myriad. You might have to go into debt for the first year or so, but as long as you plan for this, things will work out fine. Just be sure that there is a demand for what you are doing, especially if you are making a product or providing a service.'

8

'There are plenty of agencies out there who will give you advice on setting up your own business, particularly with regard to legal and taxation issues, which can be really confusing. The government in your locality probably has some kind of small business help unit and that is a good place to start.'

B Match the interviewer's questions to Antonia's answers. Fill in the gaps in Exercise A.

a _____ 'How were you able to work out whether it was viable or not?'

b _____ 'So what gave you the idea for a knitting business?'

c _____ 'So it happened just like that?'

d _____ 'Your business plan must have seemed viable then, so I guess you were pretty confident that things would work out.'

e _____ 'Now, as an ex-lawyer, you obviously have a fair amount of business acumen. Where could people go for advice if they don't have so much experience?'

f _____ 'What advice would you give anybody wanting to do the same?'

g _____ 'What made you take the plunge in the first place?'

h _____ 'Do you regret having tried?'

C Read the article again. In which paragraph can the following information be found?

1 A very important step in setting up your own business

2 Antonia's doubts

3 Antonia's goals

4 What people might need help with

5 Why she went out on her own

6 Don't aim to get rich quickly

7 The good things

8 How Antonia chose what to do

Homework

Use the expressions in Exercise D to write a test. Leave the expression blank and test your classmates next class.

D Find phrases in the article or questions which mean the following.

1 decide to take a risk _____

2 not achieving anything _____

3 it wasn't fulfilling for me _____

4 an affinity for _____

5 happy with the result _____

6 start _____

7 easily _____

8 may not be willing to _____

9 something essential _____

10 in the end everything would be alright _____

11 an unresolved thought that is bothering you; maybe your conscience or your intuition _____

12 concerning _____

13 not only that, but also _____

14 try something _____

15 the rewards are many _____

E Practise the expressions in Exercise D by discussing these questions in small groups.

1 What would you do if you trained for your career for several years, only to find that when you started, your heart wasn't in it?

2 Were you delighted with the outcome of your last test or exam?

3 What aren't you prepared to do to be successful?

4 What do you have a natural eye for? Do you think you could take up using this talent full time?

5 What do you consider 'a must' with regards to a successful life?

6 Complete this sentence: The payoffs of _____ are myriad. Now give examples.

7 Talk about a time when you just went for it and took the plunge. Did it happen just like that?

8 Are you making progress in learning English, or do you feel like you're not going anywhere?

Reading and Grammar

A Match the first half of the quotations to the second.

1 The man who does things makes many mistakes, ☐

2 There is nothing more difficult to take in hand, more perilous to conduct, ☐

3 Please all, ☐

4 When written in Chinese, the word 'crisis' is composed of two characters. One represents danger, ☐

5 Never measure the height of a mountain ☐

6 Nothing great will ever be achieved without great men, and men are great ☐

7 If the creator had a purpose in equipping us with a neck, ☐

8 Don't be afraid to take a big step ☐

☐ **a** **and** you will please none. — Aesop

☐ **b** **but** he never makes the biggest mistake of all — doing nothing. — Benjamin Franklin

☐ **c** **until** you have reached the top. Then you will see how low it was. — Dag Hammarskjold

☐ **d** **only if** they are determined to be so. — Charles de Gaulle

☐ **e** **or** more uncertain in its success than to take the lead in the introduction of a new order of things. — Niccolo Machiavelli

☐ **f** he surely meant us to stick it out. — Arthur Koestler

☐ **g** **since** you can't cross a chasm in two small jumps. — David Lloyd George

☐ **h** **and** the other represents opportunity. — John F Kennedy

B Match the quotations to the meanings below. Write the name of the person who said it on the line.

1 A risk is when you balance the possibility of a bad thing against a good thing. _____

2 Innovation is extremely difficult and risky. _____

3 You can't keep everybody happy, so don't try. _____

4 It is better to try and fail than not to try at all. _____

5 Sometimes you have no choice but to take big risks. _____

6 Success is based on a decision. _____

7 Human beings are meant to take risks. _____

8 It is only when you have achieved something that you will see how easy it was. _____

C Read the quotations again. Which ones do you agree with? Which ones do you disagree with? Which one is your favourite and why?

D What type of words are the words printed in bold? Can you sort them into two groups?

E It there any difference in meaning between sentences A and B (and C)? If so, what's the difference?

A Even if you fail, you will feel a sense of accomplishment.

B Unless you fail, you will feel a sense of accomplishment.

_____
_____
_____

A I will give you some bread only if you help me make it.

B I won't give you any bread unless you help me make it.

C Even if you help me make it, I won't give you any bread.

_____
_____
_____

A I was struggling until you came to my rescue.

B I was struggling before you came to my rescue.

_____
_____
_____

F The conjunction 'since' has two meanings. Put the sentences into two groups that use 'since' in the same way. What is the difference?

1 I've lived here since I was a child.
2 Since I couldn't take both of them, I had to make a choice.
3 We'd better call him, since he's fairly forgetful.
4 Ever since I took the plunge 5 years ago, I've been working as my own boss.
5 Since you asked so nicely, I'll do it for you.
6 Here are the records since the store was established in 1986.
7 My feelings haven't changed since we spoke last night.
8 I think we'd better call him, since he's been so helpful lately.

G The sentences below each contain an error. Find the mistakes and fix them.

1 If you don't risk anything you risk even more.
_____

2 Because I wanted to open a restaurant, so I asked for his advice.
_____
_____

3 She was terribly upset, because didn't get a call back.
_____
_____

4 Although everyone told him not to, but he did it anyway, and he had no regrets.
_____
_____

5 As you know, that I try very hard.
_____

6 I've got a friend who she started her own dance school.
_____
_____

7 I won't jump only if you do.
_____

8 The true story of what it happened to her remains a mystery.
_____
_____

9 Ever since I made the decision, so I've felt much better about where my life is going.
_____
_____

10 The exercises that we did yesterday was rather difficult.
_____
_____

Homework

Choose five of the conjunctions from this lesson and write sentences with them. Create five multiple choice questions using your sentences. Quiz your classmates with the sentences next class.

Listening and Writing

A Match the following sports to the pictures. Have you ever tried any of these? Which ones? Did you enjoy them? Why? Why not?

1 Hang gliding ☐ ☐

2 Drag racing ☐ ☐

3 Surfing ☐ ☐

4 Unicycling ☐ ☐

5 Ice climbing ☐ ☐

6 Kite surfing ☐ ☐

B Listen to the conversation between Brian and Susie. Answer the following questions.

1 What do you think their relationship is?
_____

2 Where are they?
_____

3 Where has Brian been?
_____

4 Has Susie bungee jumped?
_____

C Study the following questions. Put them in the order that the answers appear in the conversation.

_____ Where and when was bungee jumping invented?

_____ How does Brian take his coffee?

_____ How do you get back onto the bridge after you have jumped?

_____ What does Susie think about Sydney Harbour Bridge?

_____ Where did Brian go bungee jumping?

_____ How many times did he jump?

_____ What does Brian think of the centre where he went bungee jumping?

_____ How many photos did he take?

_____ Is Brian a risk avoider, reducer or optimiser?

_____ How dangerous is bungee jumping?

_____ What is the bungee made of?

_____ What is Susie afraid of?

_____ Does it hurt when the bungee stops you?

D Answer the questions in Exercise C. Interview a partner to check your answers.

E Brian uses the phrase 'to chicken out'. What do you think that means? Read the phrases below. Fill each gap with an animal from the box.

| cat | bat | owl | bee | dog | crow | mouse |
| horse | crocodile | mule | leopard | butterfly |

1 as sick as a _____
2 _____ feet
3 grinning like a Cheshire _____
4 a social _____
5 a dark _____
6 as quiet as a church _____
7 a wise old _____
8 a _____ in her bonnet
9 _____ tears
10 as stubborn as a _____
11 a _____ cannot change his spots
12 blind as a _____

F Complete the sentences with one of the phrases from Exercise E.

1 Look at John, _____. He is so smug!
2 You should listen to Mrs Jones's advice. She really is _____.
3 I had no idea you had a girlfriend! You're such _____.
4 I need to buy some new moisturiser or stop smiling so much. I am developing _____.
5 Lucia is such _____. She goes to a different party every night.
6 Without my glasses I'm _____.
7 Jackie hardly says a word. She's _____.
8 That stomach bug was awful. I was _____ all night.
9 I thought that my ex-boyfriend would act differently this time, but I guess _____.
10 She has a _____ and she won't stop talking about going white water rafting.
11 Please don't shed those _____ for me. I know that you are actually relieved that I'm leaving.
12 I tried to get Randy to come with us, but he's adamant that he wants to stay. He's _____!

G A friend of yours is thinking about going bungee jumping. You are surprised, because this is unlike your friend. Write an email giving him or her some advice. Try to use some expressions from Exercise E.

Homework

Each student should choose one expression from Exercise E and design a drawing that will help you to remember the animal expressions. Next class you can create a gallery.

Reading

A How many ways can you think of that people gamble with money or valuables? Have you ever done it? What was your experience?

B Read the article and choose the two topics that are NOT mentioned in the text.

   A Amarillo Slim's mentors
   B An anectdote illustrating Amarillo Slim's fame
   C Amarillo Slim's advice to other gamblers
   D Some of Amarillo Slim's most famous bets
   E Amarillo Slim's trouble with the law

The World's Greatest Gambler

From poker night at a friend's house to the glamorous casinos of Las Vegas, gambling is a multi-billion dollar industry. But how can you get a piece of the pie? What are the odds of hitting it big, and can you increase your chances?

Notorious gambler, Amarillo Slim, thinks you can. And he should know. Thomas Austin 'Amarillo Slim' Preston Jr. has been touted as the World's Greatest Gambler. Known to be able to win money from anyone, he once beat Minnesota Fats playing pool with a broomstick, and Evel Knievel in golf with a carpenter's hammer. He took Willie Nelson for $300,000 playing dominoes and Bobby Riggs for $100,000 playing Ping-Pong (with a frying pan!) He bet a prominent politician that Bush would win the 2000 US election, and he has won the World Series of Poker four times!

Amarillo has made a living of taking risks. Never heard of Amarillo Slim? Well, he may not be your run of the mill celebrity, but his fame has carried him through at least one sticky situation. The story goes that Slim once found himself in the middle of the hold-up of a not-quite-legal gambling venue in Florida. Along with the other patrons of the event,

Amarillo Slim was made to lie down on the floor at gunpoint. So did his reputation precede him, that as the bandits circulated the venue relieving the patrons of their valuables, one of the assailants recognised Slim and refused to take his things. Worried about what the other gamblers might think, Slim insisted that he be robbed along with all the others. Less than two weeks later, all of Slim's valuables were anonymously returned to him by mail.

So, do you fancy your chances as another Amarillo Slim? Here are our top ten tips for poker success:

1   If you can't afford to lose it, don't gamble it.
2   Be careful not to let others see your 'tells'.
3   Watch like a hawk for other people's 'tells'.
4   If you don't think you can beat them, don't play them.
5   Always be a good sport.
6   For goodness sake, quit while you're ahead.
7   Keep your wits about you: concentrate.
8   Limit the hands you play, but get in there when you do.
9   Always pace yourself.
10 Watch the players, not the cards.

C Discuss the questions with a partner.

   1 Why do you think the robbers returned Slim's valuables to him?
   2 Look at each of the ten pieces of advice. Explain what each means. Consider whether you can transfer the piece of advice to another context other than poker. Which situations can you think of?

D Find the following phrases in the text and underline them. Match them with their meanings.

1	a piece of the pie	☐
2	the odds	☐
3	hitting it big	☐
4	has been touted	☐
5	made a living	☐
6	he should know	☐
7	run of the mill	☐
8	sticky situation	☐
9	was made to	☐
10	so did his reputation precede him	☐
11	take it or leave it	☐
12	hands	☐
13	tells	☐
14	for goodness' sake	☐

☐	a	a change in a player's behaviour that gives clues to that player's assessment of their hand.
☐	b	a phrase used for emphasis as a plea
☐	c	a share
☐	d	he has the experience to back up his knowledge
☐	e	accept it or not
☐	f	rounds of cards
☐	g	was forced to
☐	h	ordinary
☐	i	difficult scenario
☐	j	earned money to live on
☐	k	has been called
☐	l	the chances
☐	m	winning a significant amount
☐	n	he made an impression on people before he met them

E Complete the table with the correct word forms.

VERB	NOUN	ADJECTIVE	ADVERB
diversify			
afford			
		notorious	
insist			
			anonymously
	value		
		situational	
			prominently

F A risk is an action that may have an undesirable outcome. Often there is the potential not only for loss, but also for gain. Study the risks list. With a partner, assess the potential losses and gains.

		Risk	Potential loss	Potential gain
1	playing your grocery money at the casino			
2	not wearing your seatbelt			
3	skydiving			
4	opening a new summer landscaping business			
5	entering a talent competition			
6	asking your crush out on a date			
7	bungee jumping			
8	applying to enter an academically exclusive school			

Writing

A Your teacher will give you some pamphlets to look at. In small groups, discuss which appeal to you, and which do not, and say why. Make a list of what is common between the pamphlets.

SELF-HELP

Good Health

B You are going to collaborate with a partner to write a pamphlet about problem gambling. First, decide who will be your target audience. Who are you writing for? Write a description of your target audience.

Social services

C Think about the purpose of your pamphlet. If your pamphlet is a means, what is the end? With a partner, define the intended purpose of your pamphlet (there may be more than one).

D Consider your target audience again. Put yourself in their shoes. What questions might they have? Write a list of at least five. Can you answer these questions?

E How much information should be new to your reader? Look at all of the information you have. Sort it into what you think is existing knowledge for your reader, and what is new information. Do you have the right balance?

F Think about the layout of your pamphlet. Fold a regular piece of paper in three. Evaluate the space you have and the information that you researched for homework. Plan the layout by considering what the most important information is, and where the most visible parts of the pamphlet are.

G Before you begin to make your pamphlet, read the following advice. When you have finished, incorporate the advice into the production of your pamphlet.

What can you use pamphlets for?

Pamphlets are an efficient way of getting information to the public. You can use them to:
- mobilise people to support your cause
- advertise a meeting or specific event
- popularise your slogans and messages

Pamphlets are very useful. They are a direct way of communicating with your desired audience, but they can also be very expensive to produce. Organisations can easily produce pamphlets but it is necessary that you are clear about who you are targeting, and what you want to achieve by doing it, before spending lots of money.

Important things to know about pamphlets

Pamphlets should be used when you want to give people more information than you can put on a poster, for example to:
- explain an issue to the community
- inform people of their rights
- gain support for a campaign you are running
- rally support for your organisation's point of view

You can produce pamphlets by photocopying them yourselves or printing them on a duplicator or by taking them to a professional printer. It is important to produce pamphlets that attract attention and make people want to read them.

How to make a good pamphlet

Before you start, make sure that you discuss the purpose, the message, the target audience and the content.
Keep your language simple by avoiding long words and jargon. The best pamphlets are short and simple. Make sure that all your facts are right. If you want your reader to take further action, be sure that the pamphlet lays out clearly what that action is, and how your reader can do it. Do not make the layout too dense with too small a font. Leave some space in between the writing either as empty white space or as space for logos or pictures. This makes it easier for people to read. Use fonts that are easy to read. You can also vary the typing by using bold and italics as well as different size letters for headings, captions and so on. Use bold headlines that catch people's attention and sound interesting.
When you design the layout do each page on a separate sheet of paper. Check spelling and proofread your pamphlet carefully.

H Meet with another group and critique each other's pamphlets. Edit word choice, grammar and spelling carefully. Make a second and final draft of your pamphlet.

I The final step in creating a pamphlet is distribution. Read the following advice. Where and how will you distribute your pamphlets?

How to distribute pamphlets

Think carefully about the target group before you plan distribution as different sectors of people gather in different places. Where are these people likely to gather? Where are you not likely to find them? Pamphlets are wasted if they are distributed in an irresponsible and unplanned way.

Handing out pamphlets at bus stops and stations is not an effective method of distribution because people are either in a hurry or have their hands full of bags. They just throw the pamphlets in the nearest garbage. It is better to ask someone in the taxi, bus or train to pass a few around so that the passengers can read them while they travel. The best way of distributing is by dropping little stacks off at schools, factories, churches or other targeted venues depending on who your target group is.

Language Practice

A Fill the gaps with suitable conjunctions.

1 I was terrified, but I realised that I either had to jump _____ look like a complete coward.

2 Jonathan loves extreme sports, _____ he is too scared to go bungee jumping.

3 Don't jump _____ the instructor taps you on the shoulder.

4 'Why do people go bungee jumping?'
'_____ some people thrive on taking risks.'

5 Sometimes they hoist you back onto the bridge, _____ sometimes a boat comes to pick you up.

6 'I will help you _____ I've finished playing with my computer.'

7 You have to choose a reputable bungee jumping centre _____ it can be quite a dangerous sport.

8 There was an accident, _____ the bungee jumping centre had to close.

9 Risk taking behaviour is part of our personality, _____ scientists think we have evolved to take risks.

10 Bungee jumping is very common in New Zealand _____ there are plenty of suitable places to jump.

C Complete the letter with phrases of encouragement or discouragement.

B Choose the best answer to fill each gap in the text.

Although the first snowboard was probably (1) ____ by M J Burchett in 1929, it was not until 1966 that the sport became (2) ____. This followed the invention of the 'Snurfer' by Sherman Popper. (3) ____ invented as a present for his daughter, Popper (4) ____ the invention and started to organise competitions using it. In 1994, snowboarding really (5) ____ when it was (6) ____ as an Olympic sport. Today, visit any ski (7) ____ and you will see snowboarders weaving in and out of the skiers on the (8) ____. It has become almost as popular a winter sport as skiing.

1 a started   b invented
   c founded   d born

2 a popular   b prevalent
   c populous   d commonly

3 a At first   b In origin
   c Originally   d Eventually

4 a sold out   b offered
   c selling   d marketed

5 a arrived   b succeeded
   c successful   d made

6 a adopted   b acknowledged
   c fostered   d accepting

7 a place   b centre
   c resort   d camp

8 a run   b tracks
   c ramps   d slopes

Dear Niki,

Thanks for your letter. Why are you so worried about the audition? It's a great (1) _____, so, just go (2) _____! I realise that it can be a long (3) _____, and they can only accept one of you, but you never know (4) _____! Only one thing's for sure, if you don't try out, you won't get the part. So don't say I (5) _____. This type of opportunity doesn't present itself too often, so I'd think (6) _____ before letting it pass you by! So just give it your (7) _____, after all, what have you (8) _____? Break a leg!

Sincerely,

Annie

D Complete the sentences with your own ideas.

1 Although the traffic was horrible, _____.

2 I couldn't sleep even though _____.

3 He only bothers me when _____.

4 I won't be able to go on vacation unless _____.

5 You aren't allowed to go out tonight because _____.

6 As it was a horrible movie _____.

7 Since you didn't come to pick me up _____.

8 You can't borrow my toothbrush even if _____.

9 I'll only let you come if _____.

10 He's going to whine about it until _____.

E Study the phrases. Choose three, and with a partner create a skit. Perform the skit for your class.

I'd think twice.	It's a great idea.	Go for it!	It's not even worth it.

What's the worst that could happen?   You never know until you try!

You don't stand a chance.   It's a long shot.   Give it your best shot!

What have you got to lose?   There's only one way to find out.

Don't say I didn't warn you.   a piece of the pie   hit it big

be touted   make a living   he should know   run of the mill

sticky situation   be made to   his reputation precedes him

take it or leave it   a sucker   for goodness' sake   the odds

F Complete the quotes.

1 When written in Chinese the words 'crisis' is _____ two characters. One represents danger, and the other represents _____.

2 Nothing great will ever be _____ without great men, and men are great _____ they are determined to be so.

3 The person who goes _____ is generally the one who is willing to do and dare.

4 If the creator had a purpose in giving us a neck, he surely meant us to _____.

5 Don't be afraid to _____, since you can't cross a chasm in two small jumps.

6 The man who does many things makes many _____, but he never makes the biggest mistake of all – doing _____.

Language Reference

CONJUNCTIONS

Conjunctions join two clauses. Coordinating conjunctions join two clauses which could stand alone. Coordinating conjunctions include 'and', 'or', 'but', 'for', 'so', 'yet' and 'nor'.

I am from France. I enjoy snowboarding.
I am from France, and I enjoy snowboarding.
I like skiing. I don't like snowboarding.
I like skiing, but I don't like snowboarding.

Subordinating conjunctions join a main clause to a clause which is dependent on it. Examples of subordinating conjunctions are 'since', 'because', 'after', 'which' and 'who'.

I go snowboarding because I like taking risks.
I have a friend who loves bungee jumping.

Sometimes, conjunctions can stand alone with one clause in informal speech.

'Why do you like playing the piano?'
'Because it's very relaxing.'

This can be because the conjunction introduces an answer, an afterthought, or is used for emphasis.

'Why did you do that?' 'Because I felt like it.'
(answer)
I don't like dogs. So I can never look after friends' pets. (afterthought)
Stop that now! Or I'll throw that video game out of the window! (emphasis)

Note that we use a comma to separate clauses that have a coordinating conjunction. For sentences with subordinating conjunctions, we use a comma to separate the clauses only if the subordinate clause comes first.

ENCOURAGING / DISCOURAGING

When someone tells us that they are considering taking a risk, often they are inviting feedback. Here are phrases that can help you give someone your opinion about their risk.

Encouragement

Do it, there is very little potential loss.
Give it your best shot!
Go for it!
I encourage you to do it.
I encourage you to take the risk because it is the only way to know if you will succeed.
I support that decision.
I think the potential gain outweighs the risk.
It's a great idea.
There's only one way to find out.
Try your hardest.
What have you got to lose?
What's the worst that could happen?
You never know until you try!

Discouragement

Don't say I didn't warn you.
I advise you to reconsider and not do that.
I think the potential loss outweighs the potential gain.
I told you it was a bad decision, so if you do it, don't complain afterwards.
I'd think twice.
It is unlikely that you will succeed.
It's a long shot.
It's not even worth it.
You don't stand a chance.
You will not succeed.

The best days of your life

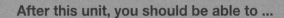

After this unit, you should be able to ...

- Understand the education system in the UK as compared to your own country
- Recognise and effectively use a range of punctuation marks and signs
- Write a personal statement as part of a university application
- Respond to points raised about home schooling in an interview
- Talk about your point of view in relation to alternative forms of education
- Recognise and use a variety of collocations, phrasal verbs, and idiomatic expressions

A Brainstorm as many words you know that are connected to 'education'. Write them down in a word spider.

B Punctuate these sentences and then compare with a partner.

1 i cant believe johns friend said that exclaimed sarah ive never heard such nonsense

2 i asked david why he said that but he wouldn't say

C Discuss these questions in small groups. Report back to class.

1 Did you wear a school uniform at school?

2 Was it compulsory?

3 Do you have an opinion about them?

4 What are the arguments for or against school uniforms?

Reading and Speaking

A What is the structure of the education system in your country? What are the key stages of school and university? Discuss with a partner the similarities and differences between the educational systems in your countries. Use the questions to help you.

1 At what age does formal education begin?
2 At what age does compulsory education end?
3 What are the stages of compulsory education?
4 How many different schools do you attend, and at what ages?

5 What are the key assessment years?
6 Are you assessed by examination or continuous assessment?
7 What different levels of university degree are there?
8 How long does each of these take?

B Read the information about the education system in the UK. How does it compare to the education system in your country?

Education Information Web

Education Information Web
Welcome to the Education Information Web, where you can find everything you want to know about the UK education system.

School Education
In the UK, education is compulsory from the age of five to sixteen. Prior to this, very young children may attend a crèche or nursery school. The basic first stage of compulsory schooling begins in primary school which caters for children between the ages of five and eleven. Primary education may take the form of an infant school (two years) from five to seven, and a junior school (four years) from seven to eleven, or may be a combined junior and infant school.

Secondary education covers schooling from the age of eleven to the minimum school leaving age of sixteen. The first year of secondary school is commonly known as Year 7. In both primary and secondary education pupils follow a common national curriculum leading to the General Certificate of Secondary Education (GCSE). During Years 10 and 11, students work towards their final GCSE examinations. Students usually study between nine and twelve subjects. These are assessed via a combination of examination and continuous assessment, with a grading system between A (excellent) and E (fail). There are many different types of mainstream state

school as well as independent schools.

If students achieve high enough grades at GCSE, they can continue studying for a further two years (Years 12 and 13). This is known as the Sixth Form (age 16-18). At some schools, students may stay on at a school sixth form or move to a specialist sixth form college. After two years they sit for the GCSE Advanced Levels ('A' levels), or vocational courses leading to General National Vocational Qualifications (GNVQ's). Vocational courses are often offered at colleges of further education. At 'A' Level, students usually study between two and four subjects of their choice. Assessment is by examination and continual assessment. The academic year runs from September to July.

Higher Education
Higher education is provided by three main types of institutions: universities, colleges and institutions of higher education, and art and music colleges. All universities are autonomous institutions, particularly in matters relating to courses. University admission is based on 'A' Level results. Most universities are divided into faculties which may further be subdivided into departments.

Non-university level post-secondary education is provided by technical colleges, colleges of further and higher education and accredited independent colleges. These offer a large number of vocational / technical courses leading to a professional qualification. The Business and Technology Education Council offers vocational courses of one, two and three year's full-time study, leading to different diplomas.

The first stage university level is the undergraduate stage. This lasts for three or four years and leads to the award of a Bachelor's Degree in Arts, Science or other fields (Technology, Law, Engineering, etc.). The Bachelor's Degree is conferred as a Pass Degree or an Honours Degree where studies are more specialised and students receive either a First, Second or Third Class Honours classification. Some universities have adopted the credit-unit or modular system of assessment. In some universities students must follow a foundation course before embarking on the course leading to the Bachelor's Degree. Sandwich courses involve an additional year's work experience. Some institutions have introduced accelerated two-year degrees which require students to study during the normal vacation period.

The second stage university level (postgraduate) is the Master's Degree, which is normally studied over one year. The normal entry requirement for a Master's degree is a good Bachelor's Degree. After two years additional study and the successful presentation of a thesis, students obtain the Master of Philosophy (M.Phil) degree.

The third stage university level is the Doctorate of Philosophy (D.Phil. or Ph.D.), awarded usually after three years' further study beyond the Master's Degree and the presentation of a thesis.

Distance learning
The Open University offers instruction for part-time study for degrees and other courses by correspondence, supplemented by radio and television broadcasts, residential summer schools and a tutorial service which operates through local study centres. There are three main types of courses: undergraduate level courses, postgraduate courses and study packs. They are offered as part of Certificate, Diploma or Degree programmes.
Many online degree courses are now available over the Internet.

Lifelong / Continuing education (Adult education)
Extra-mural education is provided by universities or other institutions of higher education to adults living in the region served by the institutions, and offer courses that are specifically designed to meet the needs of the local community. Part-time courses may be offered which provide professional updating, or leisure courses, which people attend on day-release from work or in the evening.

C Write a definition or find a synonym for each of the underlined words and phrases.

1 <u>Prior to</u> this, very young children ...
2 ... pupils follow a common national <u>curriculum</u> ...
3 These are assessed <u>via</u> a combination
4 ... <u>vocational</u> courses ...
5 ... universities are <u>autonomous</u> institutions ...
6 ...education is provided by ... and <u>accredited</u> independent colleges.
7 The bachelor's degree is <u>conferred</u> as ...
8 Some universities have adopted the ... <u>modular system</u> of assessment
9 Some institutions have introduced <u>accelerated</u> two-year degrees...
10 ... successful presentation of a <u>thesis</u> ...
11 <u>Extra-mural</u> education is provided by ...
12 ... which provide <u>professional updating</u> ...

D Discuss the questions.

1 Do you think pupils have to study too many subjects?
2 How many subjects do you think is an adequate number?
3 Choose five subjects which you think are essential and should be studied by all children. Give reasons for your choices.
4 Which was / is your favourite subject? Why?

Homework

Based on your notes and the ideas generated in your discussion, write a short essay in answer to two questions from Exercise D.

Listening and Vocabulary

A

Which one word can fill the gaps in all the phrases below?

1 _____ fair
2 rehearse a _____
3 _____ truant
4 _____ a game
5 child's _____
6 screen _____
7 all work and no _____
8 direct a _____
9 the _____ flopped
10 put on a _____
11 _____ sport

B

In pairs, answer these questions.

1 Which phrase means 'absent from school without permission'?
2 What do the idiomatic expressions 'to play fair' and 'child's play' mean?
3 Complete the proverb: 'All work and no play _____.' What does it mean?
4 To rehearse a play means:
a to practise a play
b to act in a play more than once

5 A screenplay is:
a a play that is shown at the cinema or on television
b the script for a film
6 If a play flopped it was:
a successful
b unsuccessful
7 If you put on a play you:
a produce a play
b act in a play

C

You are going to listen to an interview from a radio programme. Before you listen, match these words and phrases from the interview to the meanings below. What do you think the interview is about?

1 custodial (sentence) ☐
2 pressure group ☐
3 penal (reform) ☐
4 detrimental ☐
5 asset ☐
6 upheaval ☐
7 prosecuted ☐
8 compel ☐
9 ensure ☐
10 condone ☐
11 draconian (penalty) ☐
12 deprive ☐
13 negligence ☐

☐ a having a negative effect
☐ b overly harsh
☐ c a group with particular concerns who wish to influence public policy / legislation
☐ d a major change
☐ e to take or keep something away from someone
☐ f legal proceedings against someone
☐ g something useful or valuable
☐ h relating to imprisonment
☐ i the failure to take care
☐ j relating to punishment
☐ k to make sure
☐ l to overlook, forgive or disregard
☐ m force someone to do something

D Listen to the interview and answer these questions. Check your answers with a partner.

1 What is the name of the programme?

_____

2 What kind of programme is it and who is it aimed at?

_____

3 What is the programme about?

_____

_____

E Listen to the programme again and answer these questions. Check your answers with a partner.

1 What recently happened to a mother whose child didn't attend school?

a She was jailed for a second time

b She was fined

c She was sent on a truancy awareness course

2 How has the rate of truancy changed recently?

a It has increased

b It has decreased

c It has remained constant

3 How large was the change?

a There was no significant change

b About a third

c About a quarter

4 Which sentence best summarises Graham Howarth's opinion of the new law?

a It seems to be working well

b It is not ideal, but necessary

c It is wrong and unfair

5 How many people have been punished under the new law?

a Fewer than ten

b More than ten

c Ten

6 Under what circumstances will the new law be applied?

a Where a child doesn't go to school and the parents overlook it

b Where a child doesn't go to school despite the parents best efforts

c Where a child doesn't go to school unknown to the parents

7 Who does John Rawlings see as the victim of truancy?

a The parents

b The school

c The child

8 What two factors does Graham Howarth think are responsible for truancy?

a Poverty and parental attitudes

b Parental attitudes and low teaching standards

c Poverty and low teaching standards

F With a partner, write a dialogue which includes at least four of the words from Exercise C. Prepare to read out your dialogue to the class.

G Discuss the questions.

1 Were you happy at school?

2 What are your best / worst memories?

3 What forms of discipline were used in your school, e.g., detention, carrying out tasks, hitting?

4 Did you ever play truant?

Grammar

A Read the text about punctuation and answer the questions.

Punctuation is the use of marks and signs in written and printed texts, which helps to clarify meaning by separating words into sentences, clauses and phrases. Punctuation is an aspect of written English that is often neglected. It is assumed that it is a rigid and complicated system of rules that are difficult to learn. Furthermore, these rules are seen as petty and pedantic and so punctuation is often left out. This attitude is wrong in two respects. Firstly, the rules of punctuation are not that complicated and are easy to learn. Secondly, punctuation is an integral part of written English, and omitting it (or using it incorrectly) can be fatal to meaning.

In speech, apart from the sounds of the words that are put together, we make use of a variety of features to make our meaning clear. These include stress, rhythm, pauses and changes in tone (intonation), as well as the use of facial expressions and hand gestures. These features are not available to us in written expression, and their job is done by punctuation.

Each written language has its tradition of punctuation. There are around thirty punctuation marks in English, but only about a third of these are required to punctuate effectively. Mastery of the comma, full stop, question mark, slash, exclamation mark, ellipsis, colon, semi-colon, apostrophe, hyphen, inverted commas and brackets, will usually suffice.

1 **T F** Punctuation is a rigid system of rules and is difficult to learn.
2 **T F** Punctuation is often neglected in writing because it is seen as complicated.
3 **T F** Punctuation is to written English as stress and intonation is to spoken English.
4 **T F** Incorrect use of punctuation can make meaning difficult.

B What are the names of the following punctuation marks? Write your answers in the spaces and then check your answers with a partner.

1 ( ) _____
2 - _____
3 ; _____
4 . _____
5 , _____
6 ? _____

7 : _____
8 ! _____
9 ' ' and " " _____
10 ' _____
11 / _____
12 ... _____

C Match each punctuation mark to its use.

1	full stop	☐	☐	**a**	used to set apart a word or phrase from a sentence that is complete without it
2	colon	☐	☐	**b**	indicate direct quotation
3	brackets	☐	☐	**c**	indicates the end of a sentence
4	semi-colon	☐	☐	**d**	introduces an explanation, examples or a list
5	apostrophe	☐	☐	**e**	marks the end of a sentence
6	quotation marks	☐	☐	**f**	separates independent clauses and can replace a conjunction
7	hyphen	☐	☐	**g**	separates clauses, phrases, or items in a list
8	exclamation mark	☐	☐	**h**	indicates the place in a passage where words have been omitted
9	comma	☐	☐	**i**	indicates surprise or emphasis
10	question mark	☐	☐	**j**	used to show alternatives
11	slash	☐	☐	**k**	indicates possession
12	ellipsis	☐	☐	**l**	often used to form compound words

D The following indicates other uses of some of the above punctuation marks. Write the appropriate punctuation mark in the space.

1 used for abbreviations _____

2 indicates words used with a special significance
_____

3 introduces a direct quote _____

4 indicates a contraction or omission of letters
_____

5 indicates an incomplete thought in a passage of writing _____

E Study these lines of dialogue. With a partner write a short list of rules for punctuating dialogue.

1 'I'd like to go to a nice restaurant,' she said as they left the house together.

2 'Where's the house?' he asked.

3 Did she say, 'Meet us at three or four o'clock'?

4 'What is,' John said, 'the reason for going so early?'

5 'He shouted "Don't ever do that again!" at me,' Mark said.

F Study these sentences. Decide if either a colon or semi-colon is appropriate in each sentence, and where it should be placed.

1 She gave me the directions turn left, second right and continue until the traffic lights.

2 She had to leave the room she was feeling sick

3 He spent a fortune on her he was very rich and liked to show it.

4 I checked my equipment tent, sleeping bag, torch and waterproof clothing.

G Study these sentences which show how punctuation affects meaning. What are the differences between these sentences.

1
A woman: without her, man is nothing.
A woman without her man is nothing.

2
Bond had one problem only: Goldfinger knew he had lost his gun.
Bond had one problem only Goldfinger knew. He had lost his gun.

Reading and Writing

A English-speaking universities divide subjects broadly into Arts, Humanities and the Sciences (the Sciences are divided into Physical, Social and Medical). How do you think the following subjects might be categorised? Write 'A' for Arts, 'H' for Humanities and 'PS', 'SS' and 'MS' for the Sciences. Compare your answers with a partner.

a _____ History
b _____ Architecture
c _____ Geography
d _____ Media Studies
e _____ Chemistry
f _____ Dentistry
g _____ Education
h _____ Physics
i _____ Philosophy
j _____ Anatomy
k _____ Law

l _____ Drama
m _____ Archaeology
n _____ Economics
o _____ Music
p _____ Mathematics
q _____ Modern Languages
r _____ Business & Management Studies
s _____ History of Art
t _____ Veterinary Science
u _____ Computer Science & IT
v _____ Sociology

B If you are studying at a university, which course have you chosen? If you are not at university, which course would you choose? Add any other subjects to the list if necessary. Discuss your choices in small groups. Give reasons.

C What do you know about the university application procedure in your country? Discuss what you know with a partner.

D Discuss these questions in small groups and report back to class.

1 Who or what has influenced you to study your chosen subject? For example: family, friends or a teacher.
2 What experiences and / or qualifications do you have?
3 What are your future educational intentions and goals?

E Many universities require you to write a personal statement as part of the application process. Read the text below. What is the purpose of a personal statement? Make notes as to what specific information you would include in a personal statement of your own, based on the advice.

Writing a Personal Statement

Universities often receive thousands of applications every year. In order to help in their decisions, they require that you write a personal statement. This gives them a better idea of who you are and how rounded your education has been. From this they will be able to decide whether you have the right aptitude for the kind of course you are applying for.

A personal statement is one of the most important parts of the university application process, but also possibly one of the most daunting. Before you begin to compose your personal statement, read the instructions on the application form. You also need to show that you have done some research into the course you want to study, so it's important that you find out everything you can about it before you apply. You should also write about what you hope to gain from doing the course. Also include any career aspirations related to your choice of course. Remember, this is a personal statement, so make it personal!

Where do you begin? Brainstorm!
Make a note of anything and everything you can think of that might be related to why you wish to study your chosen subject. Next, identify your key achievements or accomplishments. Begin by listing what you have accomplished so far, and ensure that each accomplishment is relevant to your study area. These may include educational, work, social, and personal accomplishments. (When you come to write your personal statement, don't just list what you have done. Explain what you have gained from your experiences, eg. ability to work in a team, communicate well with others, given you a better understanding of your chosen subject, etc.)

Plan
It is very important to plan your statement. Most institutions set a word limit of between 300–600 words. Planning will help ensure that you include all relevant information within the word limit.

Statement structure
Your statement should follow this basic structure:

1 Introduction
It is important to begin with a compelling introductory paragraph. Write about yourself, why you want to study and who or what motivates you in your study area. A strong opening will engage the reader's attention. Try to give your first sentence an interesting angle. Avoid starting your introduction with an obvious sentence, such as 'I want to study biology because ...'

2 Body
The 'body' of your personal statement contains three developing paragraphs.
Paragraph 1 should be a short summary of your educational background in your chosen study area. What are your best academic achievements? Begin with a topic sentence (a sentence which introduces the topic of the paragraph) which links to an idea in the introductory paragraph, which should then be developed with specific detail and examples.
Paragraph 2 should be about your personal experiences in your chosen subject area. This should include why you want to study at university, what motivates or has influenced you, any extracurricular activities you have engaged in that may be relevant to your area of study (work experiences / positions of responsibility), your interests, etc. Again, begin with a topic sentence linked to an idea in your introductory paragraph and developed with specific details and examples.
Paragraph 3 should answer the question 'Why should they choose you?' This may comprise your academic abilities but also your social interests. Write about what you hope to gain from attending university, what assets you can bring to the course and your area of study, any other key skills you may have. Again, begin with a topic sentence linked to an idea in the introduction and developed with specific reasons and examples.

3 Conclusion
This paragraph will tie in all the information you have written. You want to emphasise your desire to study your particular subject. Here you can reflect on your main accomplishments and experiences. Where do you see yourself in five years time? How does the course you are applying for fit into your plans for the future?

F Using the advice from Exercise E above, write a first draft of a personal statement for a course of your choice. Remember the stages: brainstorm, plan, introductory paragraph, main body (three paragraphs), and conclusion.

Listening and Speaking

A Answer the questions.

1 What do you understand by the term 'child prodigy'?

_____

_____

2 These three people who were considered to be child prodigies. What is each person's particular talent?

Amadeus Mozart _____

Bobby Fischer _____

Tiger Woods _____

3 Do you know of any other examples of child prodigies?

B Discuss the questions.

1 What factors do you think may contribute to the development of a child prodigy (think about such factors as education, home life / parents, peers, innate ability, etc.)?

2 Do you think child prodigies push themselves to achieve so highly, or do you think they have pushy parents?

3 What particular difficulties do you think child prodigies may encounter?

4 Would you like to have been a child prodigy? Why / why not?

5 Do you have any particular talent?

C Read the following account. Which answers can you find to questions 1–3 in Exercise B?

Child prodigies have always aroused our curiosity, and their personal growth has often been the subject of historical and social interest. What, of course, sets them apart from their peers, and makes them the subject of enquiry, is their exceptional ability in a given field. What gives rise to a prodigious talent is a question many researchers have set out to answer.

Clearly, the innate talent of a child is a factor, as well as the environment that the child grows up in. A highly-gifted child would, of course, also invest a considerable amount of time and energy into developing their talent and skill. The emotional make-up and personal characteristics of the child would be further determining factors.

There are conflicting ideas about what motivates such a child. Some psychologists believe that gifted children don't necessarily have the capacity to achieve on their own, and what drives such children are their parents. Others believe that exceptionally talented children push themselves. Despite many success stories, the lives of child prodigies can be fraught with difficulties. It is believed that they often have difficulty adjusting socially. At school they will often be ostracised, have problems relating to their peers, and typically have very different priorities than them. Child prodigies may achieve great things, but there is often a significant physiological and emotional effect on their lives. Some gifted young people simply burn out or suffer mental health problems. Problems can also arise when the child becomes older and their peers catch up in terms of achievement.

D Look back at the text and underline any words or phrases that you don't understand. Work with a partner to come to an understanding. Use a dictionary if necessary.

E The words and phrases below are from an interview that you are going to listen to. With a partner, discuss their meaning. Refer to a dictionary if necessary.

prestigious	to wow someone	a strike
to opt for (something)		a lofty achievement
to play (someone) off against (someone else)		
to be like a pawn	to rave about (something)	
a big strain	in the long run	

F Listen to the interview and answer the questions.

1 What one factor is discussed that is believed to play a part in the development of a child prodigy?
2 Does the interviewee have a positive or negative attitude towards this factor?

G Listen again and answer the questions. Make notes.

1 Why did the interviewee choose this alternative to traditional schooling?
2 Who did she require permission from?
3 What benefits does she believe her child has gained?
4 What advice does the interviewee give?

H Have you, or has anyone you know, been home educated? Would you like to have been? Give reasons why or why not, describing advantages and disadvantages. Discuss in small groups.

I Work with a partner. One of you is for home schooling and the other is against. Decide between you who is for or against, and write down a list of factors to support your positions. When you have finished, work with a partner who has the same view as you and share your ideas.

J Work with your original partner from Exercise H. You have opposing views on home schooling. Use your notes to prepare to argue your case. Then hold a debate in class about the issue trying to convince your partner of your particular view. The debating issue is:

Home schooling is the best for your child.

Reading and Speaking

A Discuss any unknown words in the box below with a partner. Use a dictionary if necessary. Which of the words below do you think could be used to describe, or are connected to, mainstream compulsory education?

traditional	diverse	mandatory	uniformity
conventional	progressive	standardised	
authoritative	formal	alternative	flexible
hierarchical	institutional	democratic	rules
conformist	holistic	individuality	equality

B Study the words in Exercise A once more. Which words have a negative or positive connotation for you? In small groups discuss your ideas. Give reasons.

C The article contrasts two very different school systems. Read the article and underline the words in the text that are in the box in Exercise A.

Education for the masses?

(1) The traditional school system, as I see it, works on the principle of uniformity. It assumes that what is good for one is good for all. As a consequence of this assumption, the financial constraints and the sheer number of people involved, it has to offer a 'best fit' scenario. In order to work effectively it is necessary to have rules covering every aspect of school life; all students must adhere to them or face unpleasant consequences, usually involving curtailment of freedom.
It is also necessary to construct a hierarchy, to assume that there exists an inherent inequality among people, and to set up opposition between staff and students, and even between staff members of different levels of experience and expertise.

(2) All of this is necessary to keep the machine in good order. That is what the state school system is - a machine. Head teachers own the machines and have overall responsibility for their output; teachers are the labourers; administrators are the maintenance crew; pupils are the commodities produced; GCSEs and A-levels are the packaging which demonstrates the relative worth of the product and gives it a market value. Without this packaging the commodity cannot be sold. Because of the disaffection engendered in many students by this system, much of my time as a teacher was spent involved in crowd control and, even

worse, baby-sitting – trying to keep occupied people who wanted to be anywhere but in the classroom, so that their peers could get on with their learning. This was not what I had trained for.

(3) Despite my cynical rhetoric, I do not want it thought that I oppose the conventional system and everything that it stands for. I understand that it is a very effective system for many people – that many people need a structure in their lives that tells them exactly where they should be and what they should be doing at all times – and that it prepares young people very well for certain aspects of life outside education. The main problem I have with it is that it works on the assumption that everybody's needs develop at more or less the same age and in more or less the same way. It is a system which denies individuality, and which denies the fact that people develop at different rates and in different ways. Why does our society assume that unless people pass at least five GCSEs when they reach age sixteen, they are not yet ready for the 'real world', or are somehow inferior to the moral majority? A friend of mine left school at sixteen with two GCSEs, feeling like a failure. Last year, aged twenty-nine, he passed his law degree with second class honours and is now working in the legal department of a highly reputable investment bank. He is one of the lucky ones: for many of the young people who do not fit comfortably into society's normal expectations, the notion that they have failed can be very damaging indeed. And not just for them, but for future

generations too. Why must we perpetuate this myth that a piece of paper is the be-all and end-all of our academic careers? Surely there is more to education than that.

(4) At Sands School we do things quite differently. Firstly, we are a democratic school. That is to say that we have no head teacher, staff members have exactly the same rights as the students, and all decisions concerning life in the school are made by democratic process at the weekly school meetings. Issues are raised, and solutions sought by staff and students alike.

(5) Secondly, we encourage our students to learn at their own pace. We do currently have a formal timetable, and we do teach to GCSE. Both of these structures are in place because the students and their parents want them (they too believe the myth!). The difference is that we do not coerce students into class; they come because they want to, or because they are ready to learn. We have no bells telling us where to be at any given time, and we have no punishments for people who are not attending class. The third principal difference at Sands is that the emphasis is not on academic achievement, but on the happiness of the individual. That is not to say that we don't value academic success – it is possible to study for eleven GCSEs, though most of our students aim for six to eight – it is more a belief that it is not until young people are happy and emotionally comfortable within themselves, that they are ready to pursue self-actualisation. Many of our students (by no means the majority) come to us already damaged by their experiences in mainstream schools. They may have been bullied because they didn't fit in with society's perceived norms (either academic or social); they may have been asked to leave because of their inability to abide by the imposed rules and structures, or their refusal to do so; they may simply have been ignored or lost within the system, consequently suffering a detrimental effect on their already fragile self-confidence. In the space of just one year as a teacher at Sands I have witnessed several students enter the school extremely shy, insecure, neurotic, with a distinct lack of their own sense of worth. Within weeks they have transformed themselves into happy, confident, sociable young people. Their individuality is embraced, rather than ridiculed. They have little to rebel against, and so begin to take responsibility for their own development. Because we are a small school (about 65 students currently on roll), we are able to offer the individual attention that many young people need.

(6) I am not saying that Sands School is a panacea for all of society's ills. I am not even saying that we are the solution for everybody – there are some students who do not thrive in our non-coercive environment, who need authority to guide them. The point is that we offer an alternative. Sands School is one of a very small, but growing network of democratic schools around the world. We have to charge fees because the government continues to insist that there is only one right way: their way. The majority of our society accepts this because we are all products of the same machine, but surely education is primarily for the benefit of the individual. Its purpose is to empower us, to give us the tools we need to be able to improve our lives. There must be far greater benefits to society from happy, constructive individuals than there would be from mass-produced conformists, or, indeed, from mass-produced rebels. We must take control of our future and the future of our children. We need an alternative.

We thank Sands School, Devon, England and Martin Roberts, teacher, for their kind permission to use the article, www.sands-school.co.uk.

D Read the text again and answer these questions. Then discuss your answers with a partner.

1 According to the writer, what two things are necessary to enable traditional schools to work effectively?

2 The writer describes the state school system as a machine. Do you agree with this description? What other suitable metaphors can you think of? Explain your choice of metaphor.

3 The writer makes three points to illustrate the differences between mainstream schools and Sands School. Choose key words from the text to summarise each of the three points he makes.

4 If you could choose to be educated in a mainstream school or at an alternative school such as Sands School, which would you choose? Give reasons.

Language Practice

A Punctuate these sentences.

1   there are many factors involved in truancy including poverty educational standards and parental attitudes

_____

_____

_____

2   martin whom maria had met in 1997 was anthonys best friend

_____

_____

3   have you ever been to rome asked Frankie ive been there six times

_____

_____

4   if you liked this book and that is purely a matter of taste i can lend you another like it

_____

_____

5   martins teacher said that he was doing very well but that he could afford to work a bit harder in chemistry

_____

_____

_____

6   have you heard all the students books were stolen while they were having a break

_____

_____

7   you need the following to bake a cake a cake tin a sieve some flour eggs butter and sugar

_____

_____

8   i didn't think the book was very well written however i can see why it is a best seller

_____

_____

B What are the uses of these symbols? Do you know what each is called?

1   &   4   #
2   *   5   %
3   @   6   ^

C Change these adjectives into nouns. Choose five nouns and write a sentence with each one to show it's meaning and use.

1   traditional
2   diverse
3   mandatory
4   conventional
5   formal
6   hierarchical
7   flexible
8   institutional
9   authoritative

D Use the word in brackets to complete each sentence. You need to change the form of the word.

1   The teacher was really pleased with his _____ (present)

2   It is really important to get your university _____ right before you send it in. (apply)

3   John went to university to study _____ Engineering. (electric)

4   _____ Studies is concerned with things like global warming. (environment)

5   Which extra-curricular _____ are on offer at your school? (active)

6   What is your father's _____? (occupy)

7   We have a lot of _____ in class. I really enjoy them. (discuss)

8   In the UK, teachers have to _____ students' grades when they apply to university. (prediction)

E Match the words and phrases 1-10 to their meanings a-j. To help you, you can look back at the context they were used in the previous section on pages 92-93. You may need to change the form of some of the words.

1	sheer (paragraph 1)	☐	☐	a	make something continue
2	adhere (paragraph 1)	☐	☐	b	to force
3	inherent (paragraph 2)	☐	☐	c	to comply or conform with something
4	perpetuate (paragraph 4)	☐	☐	d	a remedy for all difficulties
5	sought (paragraph 5)	☐	☐	e	an essential part of something
6	coerce (paragraph 6)	☐	☐	f	to do well, to progress
7	abide (paragraph 6)	☐	☐	g	completely, absolutely
8	ridiculed (paragraph 6)	☐	☐	h	accept something, and act accordingly
9	panacea (paragraph 7)	☐	☐	i	laughed at unkindly
10	thrive (paragraph 7)	☐	☐	j	looked for

F Look again at the words and phrases in Exercise E. Use them to complete these sentences. You need to change the form of some of the words.

1 Despite his objections, he was _____ into signing the contract.

2 She was told by her teacher to _____ to the writing plan if she wanted to improve.

3 His parents _____ answers for his continuing poor grades.

4 He was impressed by the _____ professionalism of his colleagues.

5 At school he was constantly being _____ for his strange accent.

6 In prison you are forced to _____ by the rules.

7 Although his job is difficult, he is _____ in his new work environment.

8 There is something _____ unfair about these new regulations.

9 A move to another state school will not necessary be the _____ he hopes for.

10 History books often _____ false ideas about imperialism.

G Study the following idioms with 'learn' and 'teach'. Work with a partner and match each idiom to its meaning. Check in a dictionary if necessary.

1	to live and learn	☐	☐	a	learning something quickly
2	to learn the ropes	☐	☐	b	older people become set in their ways and resist change
3	to learn one's lesson	☐	☐	c	to learn a new job or system
4	a learning curve	☐	☐	d	you use this when you hear something that surprises or is new to you
5	to learn the hard way	☐	☐	e	to explain to someone something about which they already know more than you
6	to learn something by heart	☐			
7	to teach your grandmother to suck eggs	☐	☐	f	to punish someone
8	to teach someone a lesson	☐	☐	g	to gain from experience, especially an unhappy one
9	you can't teach an old dog new tricks	☐	☐	h	to learn from a bad experience
			☐	i	to be able to repeat something from memory

Language Reference

PUNCTUATION

1 Comma (,)

Commas are used to separate items on a list.

I went to the shops and bought some apples, oranges, tomatoes, butter, potatoes and sprouts.

Commas are also used to separate clauses and are often found before conjunctions.

The film was very well received by the press, but the Times editor didn't like it.

Commas also separate a non-defining relative clause from the rest of the sentence.

Marco, who worked as a policeman, was a tall chap.

2 Full stop or Period (.)

The full stop marks the end of a sentence which contains a statement.

The house at the top of the hill was really beautiful.

3 Question mark (?)

The question mark marks the end of a sentence which contains a question.

Do you prefer meat or fish?

4 Exclamation mark (!)

The exclamation mark marks the end of a sentence which contains an expression of strong feeling.

That is absolutely fantastic!

5 Colon (:)

The colon indicates that what follows is an explanation or elaboration.

The problem was clear: it would be impossible to open the box without breaking it.

Colons can also be used to introduce lists.

The countries represented were as follows: the USA, France, Italy, Pakistan, Thailand and the UK.

6 Semicolon (;)

The semicolon is often used to separate two clauses where a coordinating conjunction is not used.

Art is long; life is short.

It can also be used instead of commas to separate the items of a complicated list.

Examples of set phrases are fish and chips; knife, fork and spoon; right and left; apples and oranges.

7 Apostrophe (')

The apostrophe is used to denote a contraction or possession.

This is Mark's pen. These are the students' pens.

8 Dash (–)

The dash is mostly common in formal writing. Dashes are used much like colons, semicolons and brackets.

My father – a man who loves fishing, skiing and backpacking – will not be happy about the new park regulations.

Dashes are also used to introduce something unexpected and surprising.

And then we met Bob – with Lisa, if you can believe it!

9 Hyphen (-)

Hyphens are used to form compound words.

Here is a list of day-to-day tasks.

10 Inverted commas / quotation marks / speech marks (' ' / " ")

Quotation marks are put around quoted, spoken or written language.

'What do you think the answer is?' she asked.

11 Brackets or parentheses ( )

Brackets are put around material that we want to include as supplemental information.

My brother's best friend (I can't remember his name) just graduated from Harvard.

12 Forward slash or oblique (/)

A forward slash is used to show alternatives.

Answer true / false to the following questions.

13 Ellipsis (…)

Ellipsis can be used to indicate an incomplete thought in writing.

When he thought of her he began to wonder…

Ellipsis is also used to show the place in a passage where words have been omitted. If an extract is taken from a longer piece of writing, ellipsis can be used to indicate the missing sections of writing.

Language and life

After this unit, you should be able to ...

- Listen and talk about language learning
- Read for detail
- Recognise and use prefixes and suffixes
- Take notes
- Write a letter of advice

A How many languages do you speak? Ask your fellow students and survey the class. What is the minimum number; what is the maximum? Are the languages people speak somehow related, or are there people who speak languages that are entirely different?

B If you speak more than one language, which of these would you label 'foreign' languages, as opposed to 'native' or 'first' languages? How have people who speak more than one language experienced the learning of it: was it easier, more difficult, confusing?

C Do you know people who are dyslexic? Are you yourself perhaps dyslexic? What happens to people who are, and what are the difficulties they encounter? What kind of help do dyslexic people get?

Speaking and Listening

A How would you assess your own language skills at this point in your course?

	Oh no!	Pretty average	OK	Quite good, actually	Excellent
Listening					
Reading					
Speaking					
Writing					
Working with words					
Using good grammar					

My main areas to work on are _____.

B Complete the table below for yourself. Give yourself a grade from 1-10. Using key-words, write down a situation in which you might need to do any of these things, and indicate how well you think you would do.

		Grade	Situation	How well?
1	Correcting myself			
2	Asking for explanations			
3	Giving information			
4	Discussing subjects			
5	Arguing about things			
6	Describing objects			
7	Debating a subject			
8	Expressing my opinion			

C Ann, a college student, is interviewing people in the street to find out about the language they speak.

Which of the speakers ...

express an interest in learning a language _____
express a strong inclination towards a particular language _____
are too busy to learn a language _____
have succeeded in learning a language _____
express a strong inclination towards a group of languages _____
have tried, but are having difficulty learning a language _____
offer an opinion on the best way to learn a language _____
express a desire for fluency _____

D You've reached a good standard of English. How do you, personally, rate your progress to date?

1 Have you reached this level as fast as you would have liked? Has progress been easy or difficult? Why?
2 What is / was your primary motivation: work, social, studies?
3 What is your primary goal?
4 What is a good definition of fluency?
5 Is it possible to be truly fluent in anything other than your mother tongue?
6 Should fluency be the ultimate goal of the language learner? Is anything less than fluency a failure?

E You are going to hear a short extract from a question-and-answer session after a lecture. The speaker was talking about English words. As you listen, make notes under the headings given. Using your notes, write a very brief summary.

Etymology:

English uses:

Homework

Describe, in 300 words, your reasons for studying English, how you feel you are performing, what you like about the approach you are taking and what you think you need to do to become even better.

Vocabulary

A Study the words. What is the base word in each case? What do we call the extra letters? What effect do the extra letters have on the base word? Can you think of another word for each example?

enable _____

interaction _____

redevelop _____

undergraduate _____

unusual _____

B Circle the correct answers.

1 A prefix …

a comes at the beginning of a word

b comes at the end of a word

2 A prefix …

a changes the meaning of a word

b changes the word type

3 A prefix …

a is associated with adjectives

b is associated with adjectives and verbs

c is associated with adjectives, verbs and nouns

4 A prefix …

a usually affects the word stress

b doesn't usually affect the word stress

C Underline the prefixes in the words below. Does your partner agree?

disobey	illogical
irrelevant	dislike
impatient	unnecessary
unpopular	ineffective
irregular	incapable
impossible	illegal

D Study the following words. What is the difference in meaning between the prefixes in each pair?

1 unhappy   undo

2 dishonest   disappear

E Complete the sentences with a word based on those in the box. Make sure the word is in the correct form and correctly prefixed.

patient	qualify
pack	legible
veil	relevant
sensitive	honest

1 He's liar and a cheat. A thoroughly _____ man.

2 She'll say exactly what she thinks, no matter how _____ it is.

3 After the very first race, two athletes failed a drug test and were _____.

4 We all know he's lying, but do you think we'll be able to _____ his story? I don't.

5 Will you two stop being so _____! We won't be there for another couple of hours yet.

6 Sorry, you'll have to rewrite your homework. Your writing's almost _____. Take your time!

7 Could you all try to keep to the point, please? There's no time for _____ remarks like that.

8 I'm so tired. Let's _____ the cases in the morning.

F Work with your partner. Match a prefix from the left column with its meaning from the right.

1	anti-	☐	☐	a	under
2	auto-	☐	☐	b	many
3	bi-	☐	☐	c	out of
4	ex-	☐	☐	d	not enough
5	ex-	☐	☐	e	against
6	micro-	☐	☐	f	of oneself / by oneself
7	mis-	☐	☐	g	too much
8	mono-	☐	☐	h	false
9	multi-	☐	☐	i	small
10	over-	☐	☐	j	before
11	post-	☐	☐	k	again
12	pre-	☐	☐	l	badly / wrongly
13	pro-	☐	☐	m	one / single
14	pseudo-	☐	☐	n	former
15	re-	☐	☐	o	after
16	semi-	☐	☐	p	half
17	sub-	☐	☐	q	in favour of
18	under-	☐	☐	r	two / twice

G Rewrite the following sentences, replacing the underlined words. Check your answers with a partner.

> ── ■ EXAMPLE ───────────────
> *People always <u>pronounce</u> my name <u>incorrectly</u>.*
> *People always mispronounce my name.*

1 <u>I have to work too hard</u> and I'm <u>paid too little</u>!

   _____

2 Isn't that the man who <u>used to be Julie's husband</u>?

   _____

3 He's written two novels, but always uses <u>a name other than his own</u>.

   _____

4 You really <u>have too many qualifications</u> for this job.

   _____

5 When you've <u>read your essay again</u>, you'll know why I want you <u>to write it again</u>.

   _____

H Choose five more prefixed words and write sentences that demonstrate that you fully understand their meaning. Compare and check your sentences with your partner.

Reading

A Discuss the following questions.

1 Are you learning English as a second language, or third?
2 Can you give a definition of bilingualism?
3 Does bilingualism mean being fluent in two languages?
4 Does bilingualism necessarily mean that you've learnt a second language?
5 Do you already consider yourself bilingual?

B What do these words mean? Circle the correct definition.

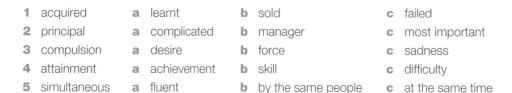

1	acquired	a	learnt	b	sold	c	failed
2	principal	a	complicated	b	manager	c	most important
3	compulsion	a	desire	b	force	c	sadness
4	attainment	a	achievement	b	skill	c	difficulty
5	simultaneous	a	fluent	b	by the same people	c	at the same time

C Read the article. How does the definition of bilingualism compare with your own from Exercise A?

Double the Fun?

Bilingualism is the ability to speak two languages with near-equal fluency. The learning of a second and of any subsequently acquired language is quite different from acquiring one's first. Except for one form of bilingualism, the learning of a second language is a conscious activity undertaken after one has already acquired the basic structure and vocabulary of one's first language. Few people ever master more than their own first language. It is only in encountering a second language that one realises how complex language is and how much effort must be devoted to learning a new one. It has been said that the principal obstacle to learning a language is knowing one already, and it may also be that the skill of learning grammar exhibited in childhood is one that is lost as childhood recedes.

Whereas almost every person masters his or her mother tongue with unconscious ease, people vary in their ability to learn further languages, just as they vary in other intellectual pursuits. The greatest difficulty is experienced by those who learn because they are told to or are expected to, without supporting reasons that they can justify. Given a motive other than external compulsion or expectation, the task is achieved much more easily. In Welsh schools, it has been found that English children make slower progress learning Welsh when their only reason for learning Welsh is that there are Welsh classes. Welsh children, on the other hand, make rapid progress in English, the language of most further education, the newspapers, most television and radio, most of the better-paid jobs, and of any job outside Wales itself. Similar differences in motivation have

accounted for the excellent standard of English and other languages acquired by people in the Scandinavian countries and in Holland, small countries whose languages are of little use in international communication. This attainment may be compared with the much poorer showing in second-language acquisition among comparably educated people in the UK and the USA, who have always been able to rely on foreigners speaking and understanding English.

Two types of bilingualism have been identified, according to whether the two languages were acquired from the simultaneous experience of the use of both in the same circumstances and settings or from exposure to each language used in different settings. (An example of the latter is the experience of English children living in India during the period of British rule there, learning English from their parents and an Indian language from their nurses and family servants.) However acquired, bilingualism leads to mutual interference between the two languages. This interference may take place in pronunciation, in grammar, and in the meanings of words. Bilinguals often speak their two languages each with 'an accent', i.e., they carry into each certain pronunciation features from the other — the German pronunciation of the English letter 'w' as if it were a 'v' or the German word order in 'He comes tomorrow home' are examples.

Successful second language acquisition, therefore, relies both on personal and external motivation. The learner should not set his or her sights too high, though. Bilingualism does not necessarily imply mother-tongue fluency.

D Read the text again and circle the correct answers.

1 The learning of a second language is ...
a achieved while unconscious
b impossible for children
c rare
d usually a deliberate, planned activity

2 The main problem in learning a new language might be that ...
a our mother tongue interferes with the process
b it's harder to remember new things when we get older
c the grammar of a second language is more difficult
d knowing one language is enough

3 The best motivation is ...
a external
b unconscious
c financial
d achievable

4 Welsh children learning English are ...
a cleverer than English children learning Welsh
b better than English children learning Welsh
c better paid than English children learning Welsh
d better motivated than English children learning Welsh

5 English speakers in the UK and the USA ...
a are helped by the number of foreigners who speak English
b need foreigners to translate for them
c are poorer than foreigners
d are bilingual

6 English children brought up in India ...
a had nurses and servants as teachers
b acquired a second language unconsciously
c interfered with other languages
d spoke with a German accent

E Find words in the article that mean the following.

1 planned and aware _____
2 meeting, finding on your way _____
3 to manage, to improve _____
4 activities _____
5 count on, expect _____

F Look at these words from the article. Are the definitions correct or not?

1	subsequently	after something else	____
2	exhibited	failed to do something	____
3	ease	lack of difficulty	____
4	justify	explain	____
5	rapid	slow and hard	____
6	account for	explained	____
7	ignorance	great knowledge of	____
8	setting	circumstances	____
9	mutual	one-way	____
10	sights	expectations	____

G Summarise the article, using all the words from Exercise E and F.

H Discuss the following questions.

1 Do you agree with the assessment of the article?
2 Were you primarily self-motivated?
3 Does your mother tongue ever interfere with your English? If so, in what ways? Can you give some examples?
4 Which have you found the most difficult in English: the acquisition of speaking skills or writing skills?
5 In what ways is the learning of speaking and listening skills different from the learning of reading and writing skills?

Listening

A When learning a language, what can hold you back from attaining fluency? Make a list of possible things.

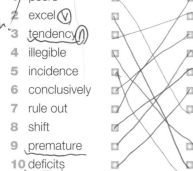

B Match the following words to their definitions.

I excel in math.

1 peers
2 excel (V)
3 tendency (n)
4 illegible
5 incidence
6 conclusively
7 rule out
8 shift
9 premature
10 deficits

a exclude something; prevent something
b the way in which someone typically behaves
c without doubt
d before the appropriate time
e change emphasis
f lack; shortfalls
g people who are equal to other people in some respects such as age, education, social standing
h impossible or very difficult to read
i do very well; be very good at something
j frequency; the rate at which something occurs

C You are going to listen to part 1 of a message on a telephone information service. Take notes, then complete the sentences, using your own words.

1 The message is about children who ...
2 If a child receives good education and still fails to develop reading skills, the child may be ....
3 Despite difficulties, many dyslexics ...
4 Specialists do not agree on a definition, but ...
5 Symptoms of dyslexia can be ...
6 Because there is no generally accepted definition ...

D You are going to listen to part 2 of the message. Correct the notes somebody else has taken.

Dyslexia

estimate ⟶ 1-2% of American population

but maybe   10-30%! ⟶ different levels of intensity – some readers affected less

diagnose ⟶ in childhood ⟶ may be genetic ⟶ research shows proof for this!

effects ⟶ only up to age 30 ⟶ most people learn to read!

girls affected more than boys!! ⟶ conclusive research data

E You are going to listen to part 3 of the message. Answer the questions, using your own words.

1 List four 'common sources of learning difficult'.
2 Describe the steps of the diagnostic method.
3 Doctors do not easily diagnose dyslexia. When do they diagnose dyslexia?

 F Say whether these statements are True or False. Listen to the whole recording once more to check your answers if you need to.

1 **T F** Children with difficulties reading, writing and spelling are dyslexic.
2 **T F** Children who are dyslexic won't necessarily be disadvantaged in their education.
3 **T F** Dyslexics may experience difficulties in areas other than language development.
4 **T F** People avoid using the word 'dyslexia' because they're not clear about what it means.
5 **T F** There is little agreement among experts regarding the incidence of dyslexia.
6 **T F** Some experts maintain that dyslexia affects different people to a different degree.
7 **T F** Research has shown that dyslexia is a genetic problem.
8 **T F** It is commonly thought that more boys are dyslexic than girls.
9 **T F** Dyslexics are often absent from school and often suffer from behavioural problems.
10 **T F** Dyslexia cannot be assumed until an intensive course of reading instruction has been tried and failed.

G The recording was divided into three sections: 1 Introduction, 2 Incidence, 3 Diagnosis.
Write the correct section numbers next to the questions.

1 Which section questions two common beliefs about dyslexia? _____
2 Which section cautions against jumping to conclusions in assuming dyslexia? _____
3 Which section cautions that doctors may have to investigate many different options before reaching a conclusion about a patient's needs? _____
4 Which section reminds us that the outlook for dyslexics need not be bad? _____
5 Which section itemises some of the symptoms of dyslexia? _____

H What sort of difficulties have you faced in your education? How did you overcome them?

Grammar

A Study the words. What is the base word in each case? What do we call the extra letters? What effect do the extra letters have on the base word?

1 Advertisement _____
2 Direction _____
3 Recognisable _____
4 Relationship _____
5 Stressful _____

B Circle the correct answers.

1 A suffix ...
a comes at the beginning of a word
b comes at the end of a word

2 A suffix ...
a changes the meaning of a word
b changes the word type

3 A suffix ...
a is associated with adjectives
b is associated with adjectives and verbs
c is associated with adjectives, verbs and nouns
d is associated with adjectives, verbs, nouns and adverbs

4 A suffix ...
a usually affects the word stress
b doesn't usually affect the word stress

C The box below contains a number of the most common suffixes. They are associated with a particular word class: noun, verb, adjective or adverb. Complete the table.

like ◁ childish (fish)
↑ selfish
foolish

er	n /adj	ee	n	ify	V	ity	n	ism	n	ish	adj
ise	V	ist	n	ive	adj	ful	adj	ment	v/n	able	adj
tion	n	ly	adv	hood	n	ship	n	sion	n	ous	adj
ness	n	al	adj	less	n/adj	like	adj	v	n/adj	ing	adj

player. *employee* *verify* *(rarity)* *mentalism* *stylish*
arise realize *pianist.* *sensitive* *beautiful* *Compliment* *Capable*
communication *commonly* *neighbourhood friendship* *comprehension* *Continuous*
illness *general* *homeless* *dislike* *dreary* *boring*

D Which word is the odd one out in each group? Why?

1 refusal - arrival - brutal - denial
2 pollution - pianist - teacher - friendship
3 tearful - handful - spiteful - beautiful
4 compliment - involvement - arrangement - appointment
5 manhood - brotherhood - priesthood - neighbourhood
6 children - childhood - childish - childlike
7 worship - kinship - friendship - partnership
8 player - singer - cleaner - dishwasher
9 goodness - happiness - sadness - forgetfulness
10 washable - edible - drinkable - terrible

E Rewrite each sentence, beginning as shown, and using the underlined word with an appropriate suffix.

1 Most of his crimes can be <u>forgiven</u>. Most of his crimes are _____.
2 The restaurant refuses to <u>admit</u> any gentleman not wearing a tie. The restaurant refuses _____.
3 Her main fault is that she's <u>lazy</u>. Her main fault is _____.
4 The company has <u>produced</u> a lot recently. The company _____.
5 She's surprisingly worried about being a <u>mother</u>. She's surprisingly worried about _____.
6 He <u>forgets</u> rather a lot these days. He's rather _____ these days.
7 He plays the <u>piano</u> at a restaurant in the evenings. He's a _____.
8 He <u>refused</u>, and that really upset me. I was really upset by his _____.
9 The government has a plan to make the capital more <u>beautiful</u>. The government has a plan to _____ the capital.
10 Can we <u>drink</u> the water? Is the water _____?
11 They really need to make the transport system more <u>modern</u>. They really need to _____ the transport system.
12 Would you like to <u>donate</u> some money? Would you like to make a _____?

F Read through the article *Double the fun*? on page 38 once more. Find all words with prefixes and suffixes, underline the prefix or suffix, and indicate whether they are a noun, adjective, adverb or verb.

Writing

A Read the excerpt from the audio exercise on pages 104 and 105. Fill the gaps with words with prefixes or suffixes.

Many children experience some (1) _____ learning to read, write, and spell. With access to appropriate teaching most of these children can and do become good readers. However, if after receiving high-quality (2) _____, a child fails to develop fluent reading (3) _____, he or she may be identified as dyslexic. A child identified as dyslexic can learn to read, but their reading often remains slower than their peers', and the effort required for reading remains (4) _____ greater. Nonetheless, many dyslexics not only graduate from high school and college but go on to excel in a wide (5) _____ of occupations.

Dyslexia is the (6) _____ to learn to read (7) _____, despite otherwise normal (8) _____ functions, but no single (9) _____ of dyslexia is accepted by all reading (10) _____. However, a central feature of all definitions is an (11) _____ and substantial (12) _____ in learning to read. Other symptoms include a tendency to write words and letters in reversed sequences, similar reversals of words and letters in the person's speech, and (13) _____ handwriting.

B Use these words to write a short article for your school newspaper about what you understand about bilingualism. Do not refer back to the unit, but use all of these words.

conscious
acquire
undertake
master
ease
compulsion
account for
attainment
exposure
interference
motivation

C You receive the following letter from a friend at home. It contains a number of mistakes with prefixes and suffixes. Circle and correct those mistakes. Check your answers with a partner.

15th January

Hi, Raoul. How are things? Everything's fine here, but it's a bit cold at the moment. I bet it's nice and warm where you are.

I saw Miguel last night. He's OK but he's been diswell lately. Garcia has a place at university: he passed all his exams but was disappointing by some of his results.

I've got some excited news, too! Mum and Dad have agreed that I can join you to study English. I'm not going to need much encouragehood! I'm arriving at the beginning of February. The flight takes 17 hours and we have to unembark in New York for two hours.

I am a little fearfull: is the England weather as bad as everyone says? Is the food really unedible?

The course startes in the middle of the month, so there will be a chance to do some sightsee. Will you be busy at that time?

I will see you in a few weeks. If you have any recommendations, maybe you can write to me?

'lipo xxx

D You are going to write a letter of advice to Filipo. Work with your partner and make notes and a plan for the letter. The letter should include the following.

1 advice about living in England (you may substitute another country)
2 advice about the language-learning process
3 advice about what to bring / what not to bring

E Write your letter. Write about 250 words. Report back to the class about what advice you would give.

Homework

Read an English newspaper and find an article that you find interesting. Scan the article for words that use prefixes and suffixes. Write the words on a separate piece of paper. Then without looking at the article again, rewrite it using the words you wrote down. Bring both the article and your report to class; let other students read both the article and your report. They can indicate whether you have used the words correctly.

Language Practice

A Fill the gaps with a prefixed word.

1 His _____ stance led him into conflict with the pacifists.

2 Stop _____! The issues are much more complex than that.

3 Do you think he wrote it himself? He wouldn't be the first person to have his _____ written by a ghost writer.

4 With the way he keeps _____, he's heading for his first heart attack.

5 He's just one of life's _____. He'll never amount to very much.

6 I've _____ this essay twice already, and now she wants me to do it again!

7 Certain animals are well-adapted to _____ temperatures. The polar bear, for example.

8 Astrology has absolutely no basis in fact. It's _____.

9 Apparently, he made her sign a _____ agreement before the marriage. He's not going to have another divorce eat into his fortune!

10 I've never heard a man with such a _____ voice. If he goes on much longer, he's going to send everyone to sleep.

B Complete the word in each sentence with a suitable suffix.

1 The policemen were sacked after being convicted of bribe_____ and corruption.

2 His humour is child_____. He should grow up.

3 Long hair used to be fashion_____.

4 He drank himself sense_____ at his birthday party.

5 He served an apprentice_____ at the print works then lost his job.

6 The President handed in his resign_____ yesterday.

7 I don't remember much about my child_____.

8 Their new album didn't live up to anyone's expect_____.

9 She's obsessed with clean_____. She showers five times a day.

10 I'm afraid there will be no pay rise for the foresee_____ future.

C Complete each sentence using an '-ing' or an '-ed' adjective formed from a word in the box.

organise   bore   bore   corrupt   exhaust   hard-work   tire

1 John is _____ and very _____, but I'm afraid he's the one we have to let go. He'll get an excellent reference.

2 I'm _____, you're _____. Why don't we turn this rubbish off and go out?

3 I'm _____. It's been an _____ day. Can't we just stay in?

4 People like him have a _____ influence on society.

D Tick ✓ the words on this list that have a prefix or suffix and cross ✗ the ones that haven't.

1 bilingualism ____✓____   6 interference ____✓____

2 unconscious ____✓____   7 imply ____✗____

3 simultaneous ____✓____   8 difficulty ____✓____

4 exposure ____✓____   9 example ____✗____

5 expectation ____✓____   10 education ____✓____

E Complete each sentence with the correct word. Circle the best option.

1 This task can be achieved so much more easily. Your approach is very _____.

a ineffective ← effective. ⇒ against.

b illegal

c impossible

d irrelevant

2 I think my remark was _____. What you say is not what I intended to convey at all.

a misplaced ✓

b misunderstood

c misinformed

d miscalculated

3 You are too _____. Please sit down and wait for your turn. I won't be a minute.

a impossible

b immature

c immobile ⇒ stuck

d impatient ✓

4 You are the biggest _____. I have ever met. Are you ever going to pass the test?

a undergraduate

b underscore

c underachiever

d undertaker

5 I must say this is a _____. I never would have thought you'd say that.

a discrimination

b disagreement

c disengagement

d disappointment

Language Reference

USING PREFIXES

dis-	the opposite of	Some dishonest operators have fooled students into buying expensive language courses.
im-	not	It's impossible to achieve that level of attainment in one year.
inter-	between or among	With language skills you improve your chances to an international career.
mis-	not or badly	The student misunderstood the teacher and had not prepared for the test on time.
out-	more than / better than	Lucy and Greg were always outperforming the other students in English tests.
over-	too much	You can't really overdevelop your language skills - the better, the more useful they are.

USING SUFFIXES

-able	verb into adjective able to be	If you speak English you'll find that people are generally very hospitable.
-ion	verb into noun process or result of	There is an onward connection from the city centre to the language school in Sao Paulo.
-ful	noun into adjective quality	There are some beautiful places to visit in Paris when you take your language course there.
-ist	changes a noun a person who does something	People who speak languages well are almost like artists: they create communication between people.
-less	noun into adjective without	The situation was hopeless for Karen: she would have to do the language course again.
-ness	adjective into noun quality of	Language schools deal in happiness: students have to feel happy.

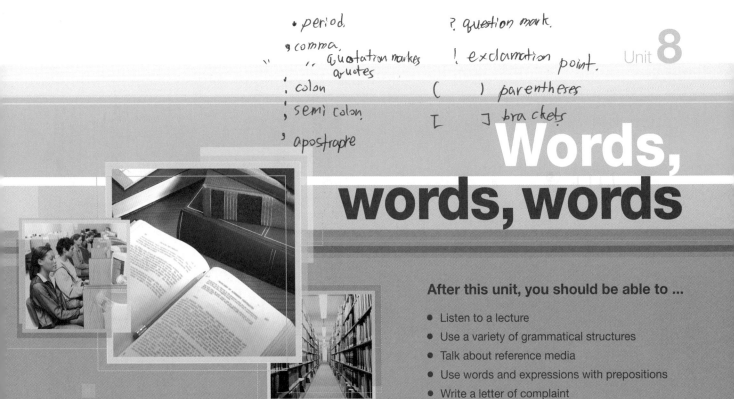

(handwritten annotations at top of page)

. period.
' comma.
" , . quotation marks / quotes
: colon
; semi colon
' apostrophe

? question mark.
! exclamation point.
( ) parentheses
[ ] brackets

Words, words, words

Unit **8**

After this unit, you should be able to ...

- Listen to a lecture
- Use a variety of grammatical structures
- Talk about reference media
- Use words and expressions with prepositions
- Write a letter of complaint

A Let's see just how long a sentence you can write. Add one word at a time following the prompts. You can change the order of the words as you write.

subject	verb	any tense	preposition
adjective	preposition	name of a place	
an	verb	adverb	adjective
this, that or these	preposition	colour	
object	plural object	verb	the	a
an	preposition	punctuation mark	

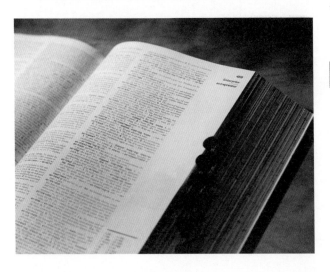

B Define these words and give examples of each.

1 noun - _person, place, ~~time~~ thing or idea. (concept)_
2 adjective - _description of noun. adverb_
3 preposition - _location, small_
4 adverb - _the manner or way something is done? How_ → _'ly'_
5 verb - _action or state of being / doing_
6 conjunction _and, but, or. / connect two clauses_
7 punctuation mark
8 proper noun
9 pronoun
10 article

C How many words do you think you know in English? How many adjectives? How many verbs? Prepositions? With a fellow student take turns counting how many words from each group can you say in 25 seconds. Your partner will count as you say them. Record the results. Compare your results with the rest of the class.

A Look at the words below. Can you write an example of each?

1 communication ⑤ syllable 5个.
2 _____ capital letter
3 _____ lower case letter
4 communication _____ accent = stress.
5 _____ noun
6 _____ adjective
7 _____ a proper noun
8 _____ a compound word
9 _____ long vowel sound
10 _____ short vowel sound

B What is the difference between a dictionary and an encyclopaedia? Try to come up with a good definition of each.

C You are going to hear a part of a lecture given at an American university. Below are the notes made by a student. Complete the notes.

Tutors: Drs Jones & Wilson

'Equivalent' is another word for a (1) _____.

The earliest dictionaries came from Mesopotamia and were (2) _____ of clay. Listed words in Sumerian and Akkadian. Others in Sanskrit, Tibetan, Hmong and Chinese. Best of early ones written in (3) _____ in the 8th c. by an Arab scholar.

Greeks & Romans will be dealt with in a (4) _____ lecture.

The (5) _____ of Calepino's 1502 dictionary included 11 languages.

Don't (6) _____! English as a world language is recent.

Early English dictionaries were for 'hard' words (7) _____.

Like Bailey, Johnson used (8) _____ to prove his definitions.

The Johnson dictionary was considered a (9) _____ for later works.

The Philological Society (10) _____ founded in 1842 and (11) _____ A New English Dictionary. Called OED —- an (12) _____ achievement.

The Webster Am. dictionary (13) _____ some English spelling.

Next: Advances in Am. lexicography and how technology has (14) _____ dictionaries.

D A dictionary is a collection of words, while an encyclopaedia is a collection of facts. Look at the following words. What are they collections of?

1 atlas

_____

2 catalogue

_____

3 directory

_____

4 album

_____

5 anthology

_____

E You are going to hear six short extracts. What are the people talking about each time?

Speaker 1	☐	☐	**a** a dictionary
Speaker 2	☐	☐	**b** an encyclopaedia
Speaker 3	☐	☐	**c** an atlas
Speaker 4	☐	☐	**d** a catalogue
Speaker 5	☐	☐	**e** a directory
Speaker 6	☐	☐	**f** an album
		☐	**g** an anthology

F Work with a partner and discuss the questions.

1 Which of the above, a–g, do you have or use?
2 Which of these do you prefer using, and why?
3 In the age of the Internet, how are these things changing?
4 Do you think the Internet will ever replace printed dictionaries, for example?

Grammar

A Correct any verb forms which are wrong.

1 A lot of homes and businesses have been being damaged by the hurricane.
2 The old theatre was rebuilding after the war.
3 I guess he will have been left by now.
4 The bridge was being repaired when I passed earlier.
5 He was being elected on a platform of transparency and anti-corruption.
6 I read the book in a single day.
7 It built in 1887.
8 The President was being visited a school when the terrorist attack happened.
9 We need to speak to John's teacher. He's being bullied at school.
10 The new bank opened by the mayor.

B Match the verb forms below with the sentences in Exercise A. There may be more than one sentence for each.

a present continuous
b passive voice
c future perfect
d simple past
e past continuous
f present perfect

1 _____   6 _____
2 _____   7 _____
3 _____   8 _____
4 _____   9 _____
5 _____   10 _____

C How are the the following tenses formed? Write the following forms of the verb 'study'.

┌── ■ EXAMPLE ──────────────┐
│ *Simple past*   *studied*   │
└─────────────────────────┘

1 Simple present _____
2 Past continuous _____
3 Present perfect _____
4 Present perfect continuous _____
5 Past perfect _____
6 Past perfect continuous _____
7 Future perfect _____
8 Future perfect continuous _____
9 Passive _____
10 Present continuous _____

D Use suitable verb forms to complete these sentences. Use the verb in brackets.

1 Tomorrow I _____ (relax) on the beach.
2 If you get back later than 8:00, Steve _____.(already leave).
3 By the end of this year, we _____ (live) here for ten years!
4 By the time I'm 40, I _____ (learn) Cantonese for 20 years.
5 I hear the European Union _____ (send) billions in aid of the flood victims.
6 _____ (you finish) that by this evening?
7 _____ (you work) over the New Year holidays?
8 If you don't get a move on, the film _____ (already start).
9 It has been reported that Gloxa Inc. _____ (spend) an additional $20 billion on research and development.
10 Sorry! I _____ (leave) in a couple of minutes.

E Fill the gaps with an appopriate verb in the correct form.

> **■ EXAMPLE**
>
> *People filled the auditorium.*
> *The auditorium was filled with people.*

1 Nobody heard from him again.
   Nothing _____ from him again.
2 An announcement of his death appeared in The Times.
   His death _____ in The Times.
3 The last I heard he was still being questioned by the police.
   He _____, the last I heard.
4 We will contact you when this matter has been dealt with.
   You _____ when this matter has been dealt with.
5 The Prime Minister has issued a statement denying the rumours.
   A statement_____ by the PM denying the rumours.

Homework

Write three short (100-word) paragraphs, using correct verb forms, about things that happened to you or will happen to you: in the past, the present and the future. Bring your paragraphs to class and compare with others.

A You are going to read about the history of the encyclopaedia. Skim the text. What do the following figures refer to? Check your answers with a fellow student.

1 1,500 _____
2 1481 _____
3 100 _____
4 1985 _____
5 1997 _____

B Read the text again and answer the questions that follow.

From Varro to Gates

The term as we know it today comes from the Greek. 'enkyklios paideia' means 'comprehensive education' and implied instruction in all branches of knowledge. This concept gave rise to the idea of collecting all the materials required for such instruction into a single work, and so the encyclopaedia (or encyclopedia) was born. The first encyclopaedia is said to have been produced in the 4th century BC by the Greek philosopher Speusippus, though no trace of his work remains.

The first verifiable work was by the Roman Marcus Terentius Varro, whose *Disciplinae* (*The Disciplines*, c. 30 BC) had nine books, though none of these survive. We have to look to the work of the Roman writer Pliny the Elder for a surviving work. His *Historia Naturalis* (*Natural History*, c. AD 77) had 37 books divided into 2,493 chapters. It remained a popular work for nearly 1,500 years.

Early encyclopaedias bear little relation to the volumes we know today. Generally, they were written by just one person and represented the sum of his knowledge alone. They were intended as textbooks rather than works of reference. In the 5th century AD, the work *De Nuptiis Philologiae et Mercurii* (*The Marriage of Philology and Mercury*, c. AD 400) appeared in verse, and in the 7th century, the Spanish scholar Isidore of Seville produced his *Etymologiae* (*Etymologies*, c. AD 623), which began with descriptions of God and the angels. It was to become the first printed encyclopaedia.

The most important of all the early encyclopaedias, though, is the *Speculum Majus* (*Great Mirror*,

1220–1244), compiled by a Dominican friar, Vincent of Beauvais. This work, which gathers together the learning of its time, consists of 80 books, including contributions from 450 Greek, Hebrew and Roman scholars. In 1481, the English printer and publisher William Caxton translated it and printed it as *The Myrrour of the Worlde*. More than any other medieval work, this revived interest in classical literature.

The modern type of encyclopaedia first appeared in the 18th century, a period of intellectual curiosity and experimentation. A trend at this time was the increased desire to make reference works useful to a wide audience. Some works continued to arrange the material by subjects, but, in general, this gave way to an alphabetical arrangement by key words, names or special topics. In this form, the encyclopaedia became similar to the dictionary, and this is the approach still employed by most modern works because it can serve both the specialised and general reader. Also, since information changes so rapidly, this approach allows publishers more flexibility in adding topics to their encyclopaedias.

The first notable encyclopaedia of the dictionary type appeared in 1674: *Le grand dictionnaire historique, ou mélange curieux de l'histoire sacrée et profane* (*The Great Historical Dictionary, or Anthology of Sacred and Secular History*). It was produced by French priest and scholar Louis Moréri, a man clearly not noted for catchy titles. What is generally considered the first alphabetically arranged encyclopaedia in the English language did even better. John Harris's *Lexicon Technicum; or An Universal English Dictionary of Arts and Sciences Explaining not only the Terms of Art, but the Arts Themselves* was first published in 1704, and a supplement 'by a society of

---

gentlemen' appeared in 1744. The text was illustrated and long remained in use.

The first of the 18th century's two greatest encyclopaedias appeared between 1751 and 1772 in 28 volumes. Diderot's *Encyclopédie ou dictionnaire raisonné des sciences, des arts et des métiers* (*Encyclopedia or Systematic Dictionary of Sciences, Arts and Trades*) was essentially an encyclopedic dictionary. It contained many articles by influential French thinkers of the day, including Rousseau. The *Encyclopédie* was considered radical by conservative elements of society, who subjected it to condemnation and its editor to persecution. This aspect of the *Encyclopédie* has given it an important place in the history of modern thought. Five further volumes with more than 200 plates appeared in 1776 and 1777. Many editions followed.

Perhaps the most lasting achievement, though, is the *Encyclopaedia Britannica*, first published in 100 parts from 1768 to 1771. It was then bound into three volumes. This work was planned by a team of three Scots: editor William Smellie, who wrote the principal articles, printer Colin Macfarquhar and engraver Andrew Bell. It contained long articles and included definitions of technical and other terms in alphabetical order. These general characteristics have been retained in each of the successive editions since the 18th century. The encyclopaedia is now in its 15th edition, published in 1974 in 30 volumes, and revised in 1985 in 32 volumes.

Beginning in the 1980s, encyclopaedia publishing expanded to non-print formats — first by using CD-ROM, then DVD and the Internet. In 1993, the Microsoft Corporation released *Encarta*, a general multimedia encyclopaedia on CD-ROM without an accompanying multivolume book set. *Encyclopaedia Britannica's* first electronic version was also published in 1993. In December 1997, *Encarta* became the first encyclopaedia to be published in DVD format.

Another innovation in encyclopaedia publishing in the late 1990s was the Internet. Online publication allowed editors to update their products much more frequently than they could when publishing on paper or on disk. By the year 2000, several major encyclopaedias, including *Encyclopaedia Britannica* and *Encarta*, were available online.

1 Why does the title say 'From Varro to Gates'? Why not 'From Speusippus to Gates'?

2 Why do you think the first paragraph offers us two different spellings of the same word? Why might the spelling have changed?

3 The first encyclopaedia was produced by the Greek philosopher Speusippus. Is this true?

4 Pliny wrote his Historia Naturalis c. AD 77. What does the 'c.' before the date mean?

5 What is the difference between a textbook and a reference book?

6 When was Isidore of Seville's *Etymologiae* first printed?

7 Who wrote *Speculum Majus*?

8 The text makes a light-hearted comparison of Moréri's and Harris's encyclopaedias. What is it?

9 What major change in encyclopaedia compilation occurred in the 18th century?

10 What advantage has the Internet bestowed upon publishers?

C Choose a topic that you and a fellow student like. Write an outline for your topic. Remember that it should have a logical order and should be interesting for anyone who would like to read about it.

Homework

Based on your outline, write an article. Bring it back into class for peer review and revision.

Listening and Writing

A What is plagiarism? Discuss this with several fellow students. Look for the word in your dictionary. What rules does your country or school have about this? How bad is it?

B Listen to the conversation. What is the situation and who are the speakers?

C Look at the list of reference materials. Listen to the audio again. Tick the ones that you hear mentioned.

1 almanac _____ ☐
2 atlas _____ ☐
3 bibliography _____ ☐
4 biographical source _____ ☐
5 chronology _____ ☐
6 compilation _____ ☐
7 dictionary _____ ☐
8 directory _____ ☐
9 encyclopaedia _____ ☐
10 handbook _____ ☐
11 index _____ ☐
12 abstract _____ ☐

☐ a contains information about words, grammar
☐ b assists in providing information about a book such as author and publisher
☐ c summarises the contents of a larger work
☐ d gives information about individual people
☐ e information about people or organisations arranged in a specific type of order
☐ f concentrates on a specific subject area
☐ g allows a user to access various points
☐ h collection of facts about many subjects or just one subject and may be one or more volumes
☐ i collections of documents or excerpts of texts
☐ j dates and timelines for topics and events
☐ k topographic and geographic information
☐ l a general reference source that includes brief information about people, nations, specific events

Now match the words to the definitions on the right.

D Write or find five 'difficult' sentences and have a fellow student try to paraphrase them. Check their work to see that the ideas are the same as in your original ones.

1 _____

2 _____

3 _____

4 _____

5 _____

E In groups, discuss the questions and report back to class.

1 Do you have any experience with plagiarism, either through yourself (be honest!), fellow-students or friends / relatives?

2 Do you think plagiarism is a typically Western concept? Do other cultures make less of an issue of it?

3 What would you say if a fellow-student came up to you and confessed to plagiarism?

4 What kind of information are people not permitted to copy?

5 How does paraphrasing help?

6 Are translations a form of plagiarism?

7 What other ways are there of referring back to a source you have used? What are the general guidelines for this? (You may have to do some research on this?)

Homework

Write two paragraphs about two topics that interest you. You are allowed (for once!) to plagiarise one of the paragraphs, but the other paragraph has to be completely in your own words. Bring both of them into class, let others read them and see whether people can discover the plagiarised paragraph. Find out what made them discover the truth.

Vocabulary

A Choose the most suitable word from the list below to complete each sentence. Remember, if you choose a verb, the form may need to change.

irrespective	capable	see
disregard	earmark	appeal
exception	cater	prone

1 Peregrine showed a complete _____ for the safety of the others.
2 We _____ to the needs of our customers as our top priority.
3 You want me to help you? Sorry, I think you're perfectly _____ of washing the dishes yourself.
4 Well, you could try _____ to his better nature, but I don't think he has one.
5 I'm going to buy three, _____ of the cost!
6 Murder? That man's _____ of anything.
7 I'm afraid this is an _____ to the rule.
8 I wouldn't believe everything she says. She's _____ to stretching the truth a bit.
9 I hear John's been _____ for promotion.
10 You sit down. I'll _____ to the children.

B Discuss with a fellow student the meanings of the expressions in italics.

1 She felt *at sea* on her first day at her new job.
2 The police are not sure if the fire was started *by accident*.
3 Bats don't come out *by day*.
4 You can only learn to swim *by degrees*.
5 Actors need to learn their lines *by heart*.
6 I know Jack *by sight*.
7 *By rights* you should be doing this job.
8 I knocked at your door *by mistake*.
9 I saw Harriet *by chance*.
10 His explanation did not put our minds *at rest*.

C Complete the sentences so that they show the meaning of the phrases from Exercise B.

1 *She felt at sea on her first day at her new job so she started to cry from frustration.*
2 The police are not sure if the fire was started by accident _____.
3 Bats don't come out by day _____ _____.
4 You can only learn to swim by degrees _____.
5 Actors need to learn their lines by heart _____.
6 I know Jack by sight _____ _____.
7 I saw Harriet by chance _____ _____.
8 His explanation did not put our minds at rest _____.

D Rewrite each sentence so that it contains the word in capital letters and the meaning stays the same. Check your answers with your partner.

> **■ EXAMPLE**
> *I'll look after the children. SEE*
> *I'll see to the children.*

1 Suddenly I just had to have some chocolate. CRAVING
_____

2 You can't reach the village in the winter. ACCESS
_____

3 He was found guilty of burglary. CONVICT
_____

4 I really don't care about her problems. INDIFFERENT
_____

5 He will be able to apply for a driving licence soon. ELIGIBLE
_____

E Fill the gaps with the preposition that goes before each expression.

1 _____ the circumstances / no circumstances / an obligation / pressure / suspicion

2 _____ breath / the ordinary / pocket / all proportion

3 _____ all likelihood / collaboration with / recognition of / favour of something

4 _____ approval / average / a regular basis / the verge of

F Complete each sentence with a suitable expression from Exercise E.

1 He wrote the musical _____ two other people.

2 I don't know what upset her. She ran out _____ tears.

3 I'm 100% not _____ capital punishment. It's wrong.

4 She had been working for the company as a temp, but now they've asked her to work _____.

5 We had the sofa _____ for a month, but we've decided to send it back.

6 That hill is really steep. Can we sit down? I'm really _____.

7 _____ are the children allowed to watch that film. It's too violent.

8 With this takeover happening, he's been _____ for a long time. I hope he gets a chance to take a break soon.

9 _____ your 25 years service here, I'd like to present you with this watch.

10 Here's a little more money. I don't want you to be _____.

Writing and Speaking

A You are going to do a research-based project. Choose a topic and then use the questions below to help you decide the scope.

1 What question are you trying to answer in your research?
_____

2 Have you narrowed your topic or is it still very general?
_____

3 What does your group already know about the subject?
_____

4 What Internet or other sources will you use? Is there more than one type?
_____

5 What writing tools will you use to make sure that you don't make mistakes?
_____

6 How will you avoid plagiarising?
_____

7 How do you plan on organising the information?
_____

8 Does all the information relate to the topic?
_____

9 Prepare an outline of your topic.
_____

B Exchange outlines with another group. Give them your opinions and suggestions. Revise your outline, using the feedback you received.

C For this project you are going to choose a family member, a friend or a teacher as your subject. Follow the steps below.

1 Step 1
a Write as much information as you can about the person you chose.
b Write down everything you know about his / her hobbies, accomplishments, etc.
c Organise the information into categories. For example, accomplishments: my father has written three books on 'endangered species of USA'.
d Create a timeline of the person's life and include all major events.

2 Step 2
Imagine that you are going to publish your person's information so that it can be read by everyone. Make a list of all the reference books in which all your information will appear and exactly what info would appear in them.

3 Step 3
Decide on key words that people might use in order to find the information in different sources.

> ■ EXAMPLE
>
> _subject: John F. Kennedy_
> _key words: American presidents, President assassinated, etc._

D Prepare a presentation for the class showing how you have successfully cross referenced your subject's information. Explain your research steps. You may prepare a diagram illustrating the process. Finish off your presentation by reading aloud the short but complete biography about your person.

E Write questions to ask your fellow students about their presentations to check if they have cross referenced their information well, and used as many reference books possible.

F You are going to give your fellow student a grade. You must be fair on them. Answer the following questions about their work. Then give them a grade.

Grading Criteria

A = Every step was taken and clearly accounted for (see Exercise A). The information was clear and relevant. A great part of the work was written in his / her own words.

B = Most of the steps were taken, most of the information was relevant, most of the work was written in his / her own words

C = He / She skipped some steps, the research was not complete, the information was not really relevant, suspect a good amount was not his / her work

D = The research was very weak, therefore was not relevant and not interesting.

Tick off the following to help you decide on the grade:

1 Was a question answered?
2 Was the topic narrowed down?
3 Was the topic made interesting for the class?
4 Were sufficient sources used?
5 What kind of mistakes 'if any' were made?
6 Did he / she avoid plagiarising?
7 How was the information organised?
8 Was all the information relevant?
9 Was there a clear outline?
10 At the end, did you feel that you learnt a lot about the topic?

G Write your biography up for homework.

Language Practice

A Put each verb in brackets into an appropriate form.

Students, as we all (1) _____ (know), tend (2) _____ (obsess) about grammar. It (3) _____ (be) surprising. In the past, schools (4) _____ (spend) a great deal of time drilling grammar at the expense of other equally important language elements. Isn't vocabulary just as important? If the grammar of a sentence (5) _____ (be) wrong, you may still be understood. But if the words are all wrong, you (6) _____ (never make) yourself clear.

Thankfully, the days (7) _____ (go) when students (8) _____ (chain) to desks, (9) _____ (recite) lists of irregular verbs by rote. Yes, those verbs (10) _____ (be) important, but it's a waste of time if the student isn't able to use them. Language is about communication and it is the fear inherent in this that (11) _____ (hold) most students back, not their lack of grammar.

(12) _____ (listen), guys. Stop (13) _____ (be) so nervous. Last night while you (14) _____ (pore) over your books, trying (15) _____ (memorise) yet another grammatical structure, others were out actually (16) _____ (use) the language. OK, so what if they (17) _____ (make) a mistake or two? The student who never opens his or her mouth will never make a mistake, but that student (18) _____ (not get) very far in life, either.

The teaching of language (19) _____ (change) dramatically over the years, but what (20) _____ (not change) far enough yet is the way students approach the learning process. Teachers must be sympathetic, though. There is huge parental pressure for students (21) _____ (succeed) in exams, and exams still mark language as right or wrong. But, (22) _____ (bear) this in mind. The students who invariably do best at exams are those with a good and confident grasp of the language. Confidence – that's the key. Maybe you should (23) _____ (go) out last night and (24) _____ (meet) some new people in a relaxed situation instead of (25) _____ (sit) at home with those verb lists! Think about it!

B Put a tick (✓) next to the sentences if you think the preposition has been used correctly. Correct the preposition if you think it is incorrect.

1   He swam across the English Channel at the age of nine.

2   He wasn't injured except for a cut above his left ear.

3   She walked in among her two bodyguards.

4   I'm not saying he's stupid, but he doesn't have much between his ears.

5   He was so short he could hardly see through his desk.

6   He hasn't cleaned properly. He just swept the dust below the rug.

7   Looking out from the tower, the view behind us was breathtaking.

8   Java lies between the islands of Sumatra and Bali.

9   The coin rolled in the table.

10   I ate too much on lunch.

C Write sentences with the following prepositions.

1   verb + 'at'

_____

2   verb + 'into'

_____

3   adj + 'of'

_____

4   adj + 'for'

_____

5   adj + 'to'

_____

6   verb + 'with'

_____

7   adj + 'in'

_____

8   adj + 'about'

_____

9   verb + 'over'

_____

10   verb + 'for'

_____

D Explain why the verb forms in these sentences are in the correct tenses.

1   John went to school yesterday with his brother.
2   I haven't seen Harriet since last year.
3   When I was a little girl I used to ride my bicycle to school.
4   While my mother was cooking I was ironing.
5   The thief was caught right outside the bank.
6   John was elected president for the fourth time in a row.
7   If I were a millionaire I would buy a very expensive house.
8   The people were angry at the governor.
9   If you heat water it boils.
10   I have been studying Japanese for 2 years.

E Complete these paragraphs with the correct prepositions.

I really like buying things that are made (1) _____ hand because I can appreciate all the dedication of the person that worked (2) _____ them. Since we are not familiar (3) _____ the origin of things we don't really become attached (4) _____ them.

I went to the Caribbean because I was tired (5) _____ my stressful job and life. I chose Cuba because I was interested (6) _____ the history behind Castro's Regime. I knew that it wasn't going to be similar (7) _____ any place I had ever gone to. I was, however, worried (8) _____ the political situation of the island. I was aware (9) _____ the poverty. When I came back I had more respect (10) _____ the pride Cuban / Americans still showed even far away from their island.

Language Reference

VERB FORMS

The forms of the verbs tell you when events take place.

the verb 'study'

Present Simple	Past Simple	Future Simple
study / studies	studied	will study
Present Perfect	Past Perfect	Future Perfect
has / have studied	had studied	will have studied
Present Continuous	Past Continuous	Future Continuous
is / am / are studying	was / were studying	will be studying
Present Perfect Continuous	Past Perfect Continuous	Future Perfect Continuous
has / have been studying	had been studying	will have been studying

PASSIVE

Sentences can also be in the passive verb form. The passive verb form too has its own tense forms.

the verb 'help'

Passive: Simple Present	Passive: Simple Past	Passive: Present Continuous
is / are helped	was / were helped	is / are being helped
Passive: Past Continuous	Passive: Present Perfect	Passive: Past Perfect
was / were being helped	have / has been helped	had been helped
Passive: Future Perfect	Passive: Future	Passive: Future with going to
will have been helped	will be helped	is / are going to be helped

PREPOSITIONS

Prepositions: are words that express a relationship between a noun or pronoun to other words in a sentence. In this unit we have seen how prepositions can be part of a phrase with a verb or another part of speech. When they do so, they are called prepositional phrases and can act as an adjective or adverb or a verb. It is important to memorise as many as you can.

NOUNS and PREPOSITIONS	ADJECTIVES and PREPOSITIONS	VERBS and PREPOSITIONS
approval of	afraid of	apologise for
awareness of	angry at	ask about
concern for	aware of	ask for
confusion about	capable of	belong to
hatred of	careless about	bring up
hope for	familiar with	care for
interest in	happy about	find out give up
love or need for	interested in	grow up
participation in	jealous of	look for

Appendix

iLab links

Unit 1 Advertising

Have you ever placed an advertisement in the classifieds? Would you if you had something to sell? In small groups discuss these questions and brainstorm which items are commonly sold secondhand and whether you would buy them or not. Then think of several items that you brought with you from home that you don't use but would like to get rid of. In the iLab class you are going to write several classified advertments for your unwanted belongings.

Steps:

1   Choose three or four personal items that you would like to sell for a profit.

2   Look at some websites from local newspapers and pay attention to how the ads are structured (ie. brief description, price etc).

3   Write up ads for the chosen items. Remember that the ads should be persuasive enough to convince your classmates to buy your unwanted goods. Each ad should be about 30 words long.

4   Print out the ads on one piece of paper.

5   In class, pass the ads around the room and see who can sell the most items or who can make the most money.

6   Discuss why some ads work while others don't.

Unit 2 The environment

Is the city you are in environmentally friendly? In your iLab class, do a search for environmental groups in the country you are in, related to any of the topics from the unit (eg. endangered species or pollution). Choose one that interests you the most and take notes about the organisation and its cause(s). Be sure to include information about what its major concerns are and how it is trying to combat/improve the current situations.

1   What is the name and focus of the organisation?

2   What are some current issues they are involved in? Domestically / Internationally

3   Choose one of the issues that concerns you and record some facts about it.

4   What is being done?

5   How can local citizens become involved?

In small groups of three or four each person takes a turn at presenting the topic they have chosen. This could then lead to comparison and contrast of the organisations.

Follow-up activity:

Write a leaflet to promote the group or discursive composition giving facts and opinion on an issue.

Unit 3 What's in the news?

What is a 'big' story in the news today? In this iLab link, you will compare different news sites' reporting of the same story, and determine some reasons for these discrepancies.

Steps:

1 Using a search engine, enter your chosen news story.
2 Search at least three different types of news sites (try to find a variety of sites).
3 Search at least two blog sites (blog = a personal web log/personal opinion site).
4 Copy and paste the articles of your choice into a word document, and print it out.
5 Make notes (in your own words) on the articles keeping in mind the following questions:
   a Who is writing the news?
   b For whom is the news written (who is the intended audience)?
   c What is the writer's perspective (politically, nationally, etc)?
   d What is the 'tone' of the article (sarcastic, conservative, liberal, etc)?
      What language is being used to imply this tone?
6 Prepare a presentation for the class: Which article do you believe to be the most 'true'? Explain your decision using your notes and examples from the articles. Share your articles and examples with the class.

Unit 4 Medical matters

Below are some common idioms that include parts of the body. You're task for this iLab link is to search the Internet for the real meanings of the idioms and give correct examples for each.

1 to bad-mouth somebody
2 'break a leg!'
3 to drag one's feet
4 to get out of hand
5 to face the music
6 'finger lickin' good'
7 to keep your chin up
8 to let your hair down
9 to learn STG by heart
10 to get off on the wrong foot

There are many sites that have helpful information about idioms so don't forget to write down the website addresses of the best sites to share with your classmates.

Follow-up activity:

Compare your findings with a partner. Then in pairs or small groups, write a short story including the idioms to demonstrate your understanding. The stories could then be passed around or read aloud.

iLab links

Unit 5 Risky business!

Extreme sports are very popular among thrill-seekers. In this unit, you have discussed many activities, such as bungee-jumping and skydiving. But where do these sports come from and why do people start doing them?

Choose one of the following extreme sports or write about the one your teacher gives you. If you have done one of the following, write about your experience.

BMX biking	Mountain biking	Whitewater rafting	Cave diving	Urban kayaking
Motor cross	Parkour	Skydiving	Extreme skiing	Zorbing
BASE jumping	Storm chasing	Big wave surfing	Kite surfing	Whitewater kayaking
Drag racing	Gravity Games	Rock climbing	Scuba Diving	Sky surfing

Go to www.google.com and type your sport into the search field.

Write a 150-to 200-word report (using your own words) about the sport, answering the following questions:

a What does your sport involve (e.g. equipment, specific area, etc.)?

b Who usually does this sport (e.g. age range)?

c Why do people do it?

d How much does it cost?

e What are the risks involved?

f Would you try or have you ever tried this sport?

When everyone has finished, present your extreme sport to the rest of your classmates.

Unit 6 The best days of your life

Trying to find out information about studying abroad can be a daunting and confusing task. Thankfully, these days, all the information you need about the schools is on the Internet. In this iLab link, you are going to use these online services to inform yourself about one particular institution in your area.

Steps:

1 Your teacher will assign everyone in the class one school to research. Among these will be a variety of local trade and technical schools along with universities and colleges.

2 Find out as much information as you can for international students on the following areas:

a Application process and fees

b English assessments and testing

c TOEFL scores

d Types of programs (degree/certificate/ diploma)

e Housing

f Location

g Course fees

h Services

3 Take notes on each area and bring them to class.

4 In class, your teacher will divide you into small groups in which you will be able to share and compare the information together.

Follow-up activity:

Discuss how useful the institution's websites were including both positive and negative features.

Unit 7 Language and life

A language can be described as a living, breathing thing that is constantly changing and adapting to its environment. From one generation to the next, language is in a constant state of development that reflects the changes to the world around it.

Learning a second language is now considered to be a marketable asset, but while relatively easy for some, it can be extremely difficult for others. Expectations and abilities vary from person to person. There are different theories as to why this may be.

Choose a topic from the list below and research the theories behind the idea.

a Innate language learning

b Language acquisition

c Language assimilation

d Multilingualism

e Bilingualism

f Changes in the English language

Go to www.google.com and enter the topic into the subject line. You may need to search several sites in order to get a full understanding of your topic.

Develop your research into a short lecture to give to your class. You may include handouts (pre-prepare and give to your teacher to be copied), visual aids (charts, graphs, overhead projector if available) or a list of key vocabulary to help the class better understand your topic.

Unit 8 Words, words, words

Maps, and how we create them, affect how we see and navigate our world. From early exploration and nation building to mapping the genes of the human body, maps help us to find our way in the vast universe of information in which we live. In this iLab link, you are going to research and summarise one of the many styles of cartography (map drawing) in the world today.

Steps:

1 Go to a search engine of your choice and enter one of the following in the search window:

a MRI mapping

b Green maps

c Cybergeography

d News maps

e VisuAide – maps for the blind

f Aerial maps

g The Peters Projection

h Satellite maps

2 Survey the sites available and take notes on the following information:

a the history / origins of this style of cartography

b it's purpose

c how it's made

d short- and long-term consequences for people / the planet

3 Write a summary of your findings and present it to your class. Use visual aids (overhead projector, pictures, graphs, charts), handouts, or realia (real objects such as magazines, pictures, posters, etc) as desired.

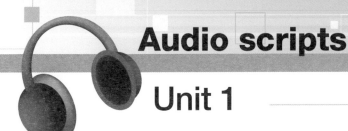

Page 2 Exercises B, C & E

Presenter: Advertising is perhaps one of the most controversial topics in today's society. We are constantly bombarded by images on billboards and posters when outside, and the advertisers come into our houses through our televisions, radios and magazines. We are quite used to this situation now, and as a society have come to accept it, but recently it has been suggested that advertising should be allowed in an area which has until now been sacrosanct, and that is the school. With me in the studio I have James Brown, an expert on education, and joining us from the United States is Professor Pauline Acton, who has been studying this area for a few years. Pauline, can I turn to you first? Advertising in schools has been possible in the United States for quite a few years now if I am correct?

Pauline: That's right, although it is something we have been seeing increasingly since the late 1990s. This is when some schools started to cooperate with companies to allow direct advertising in schools. This has taken many different forms. One of the first instances was where a multinational company distributed free books to schools in return for being able to place their logo on the cover. We are all familiar with the role that advertising and sponsorship play in sport and this has recently begun to enter the world of school sports, with a number of homecomings having been sponsored by large soft drinks and sportswear companies.

Presenter: So what is it that leads schools to agree to, or even seek these deals with companies?

Pauline: From the schools point of view there are many financial and economic benefits to the advertising. As I said before, one of the first projects was to supply free books which benefited the school concerned greatly. You are finding now that some companies are offering schools commission on sales of products advertised and sold in their schools, which is the first example of direct income generation for schools.

Presenter: So James, advertising can bring in revenue for cash-starved schools. That sounds like something that would appeal to an awful lot of institutions in this country.

James: Yes, indeed. Government spending in all areas has become increasingly hard to come by in the last ten years, and many schools are finding it hard to maintain their buildings as well as buying educational materials, so this is something that local authorities are becoming interested in. What concerns me however, is that this advertising will be done responsibly. We would all be shocked if cigarettes or alcohol were to be advertised to school children,

yet in the US a large number of adverts in schools are for soft drinks and junk food, such as crisps, hamburgers and pizza, which could have an equally destructive affect on the health of our young people.

Pauline: It is true that certain fast food companies advertise in schools, but these advertisements tend to be quite subtle, and they are brands to which the students are exposed to and are quite familiar with outside school. Sometimes, it is just a case of a particular product being sold in the school cafeteria which is a form of indirect advertising which I am sure has been around in UK schools for a long time.

James: This is true. Chocolate bars, crisps and fizzy drinks have been available in cafeterias and tuck shops for a while. Going back to Pauline's point about these brands already being familiar to students for a moment, I think there is a problem with advertising products in school which is unique to them. The school environment is one which carries a great influence and authority. Advertisements which appear to have the school's backing may therefore carry a greater weight as schools tend to be respected institutions.

Pauline: Studies in the US have indeed shown that this is the case, so it is up to school boards to think very carefully about this. On the whole however, there do not seem to be too many problems developing.

James: I don't quite agree with that point. Both in the UK and US instances of child obesity are on the rise, and the advertising of junk food could be contributing to that. One further problem is that children in school are a captive audience. At home, they can turn the TV off, or their parents can, and advertising can be avoided. This is not the case in schools.

Presenter: So, what kind of regulation can we expect within UK schools?

James: Well, currently advertising in schools is allowed at the discretion of the Head teacher and governors who are obviously accountable, and we do have very effective bodies such as the Advertising Standards Agency, who regulate adverts generally. It is early days so far and so we will have to wait and see what further regulation is necessary, if any, in the future.

Presenter: Well, I think it sounds like an experiment which could benefit schools greatly if carried out responsibly and that is, I'm afraid all we've got time for now, so I would like to thank my guests ...

1   Worried about your weight? Don't seem to be able to shift
    those stubborn pounds you put on over Christmas? Well help
    is on its way in the form of Ultraslim. Our new weight loss
    system could help you lose up to 4 lbs per week. Follow these
    simple instructions: For breakfast, have one of our delicious
    milkshakes, have an Ultraslim bar for lunch, and then eat an
    ordinary meal in the evening. You will be looking good and
    feeling good in no time. Our advanced slimming formula can
    also help you to avoid high blood pressure and heart disease.
    So, don't wait to lose that weight! Get Ultraslim today.

2   A luxury vehicle unlike any other, the Dacona 500 series GTI is
    the car for today's man about town. Its leather lined interior and
    state of the art entertainment systems mean that driving will
    be a pleasure you won't want to miss. Our new ergonomically
    designed wheel, gear stick and controls will leave you feeling
    as relaxed and comfortable as if you have just got out of
    bed. Extra space has been devoted to the boot area, so big
    shopping trips or taking the family on holiday will never be a
    problem. The new Dacona 500 GTI. The car you won't want to
    get out of driving.

3   Make dry, greasy hair a thing of the past, with new Dazzle
    shampoo for women. As well as leaving your hair with that
    squeaky clean feeling, our new Norwegian formula can actually
    stimulate hair growth, leaving your hair thicker and healthier
    than ever before. So, next time you are having a bad hair day,
    don't reach for a hat, reach for new Dazzle Norwegian formula,
    for hair you will be proud of!

4   Megan: Hey, Jackie? What's that you're drinking?
    Jackie: It's new Cranberry Crush. Try it!
    Megan: Hey, that tastes great, just like fresh
              cranberry juice.
    Jackie: I know, you can hardly taste the vodka!
    Megan: Fantastic! Sounds like we are in for a good
              night then!
    Voice: Cranberry Crush, no taste of vodka,
              just the rush!

Audio scripts

Unit 2

Page 20 Exercise C & Page 21 Exercise D

Welcome, and in today's lecture we are going to continue looking at the theme of pollution and in particular one of the effects that air pollution has on our weather. We are going to look at acid rain, which is one of the major ways in which air pollution is transferred to other parts of the environment. I will begin by looking at what acid rain is, before moving on to what causes it. Then I shall have a look at the effects which it can have on the environment at large. Finally, I shall look at how it can be prevented.

So what exactly is meant by acid rain'? Scientists refer to acid rain as 'acid deposition' which has two main forms, wet and dry. Wet deposition refers to rain, fog and snow which contains quantities of chemicals. Dry deposition on the other hand refers to gases and particles which are exuded into the atmosphere. These then fall back down to earth or are absorbed from the air into objects, buildings and breathed in by animals. The shared characteristic of both of these kinds of deposition is that they are invisible. I don't mean that you cannot see the rain, snow or fog of course, but we do not see the chemicals they can contain.

Acid depositions can travel many thousands of miles on the prevailing winds and so are something that can affect the environment a long way from the source of the pollution.

So what causes acid depositions? Analysis of the atmosphere suggests that two chemicals are mostly responsible for acid deposition today. These are sulphur dioxide and nitrogen oxide. Although both of these chemicals exist in the atmosphere naturally, about two thirds of atmospheric sulphur dioxide and a quarter of nitrogen oxide can be traced to the burning of fossil fuels which is central to our electricity production industry. These gases will react with the weather system to produce mild forms of sulphuric and nitric acid in rain, fog and snow.

So, what affect does all of this have on the environment? Well, firstly, acid depositions both dry and wet can be absorbed into the water table which provides drinking water for all living creatures, ourselves included. But, this will also lead to it getting into the food chain generally as plants and animals are affected by it. In extreme circumstances it can lead to the destruction of plant and animal life when concentrations of acid are particularly high.

Acid depositions can also affect the urban environment. As rain and dry depositions come into contact with buildings they can cause serious erosion, which not only means that we need to expend new resources in repairing them, but that sometimes our historical and cultural heritage is put in danger. Metal and paints, particularly those which make up parts of cars are also heavily affected by acid depositions.

It would be almost impossible to stop acid depositions without completely moving back towards a pre-industrial society, so I am afraid that this problem is one which is likely to be with us for a while. However, by attempting to move away from the burning of fossil fuels and looking for cleaner forms of energy we might be able to minimise its effects.

Next week we will move onto looking at the so-called 'greenhouse gases', but before I finish, do we have any questions?

Judy: Did you know that in Britain each year, we consume six million cans of fizzy drink, twelve billion tins of food and use two tree's worth of paper each? And, what's worse is that we end up throwing most of it away. As a result, the UK produces twenty-five million tonnes of waste every year, about three quarters of a tonne per head of population! This has finally lead to an increase in the amount of recycling that we are all doing but is this worth it or just a waste of time and energy? To help us find out, I am joined in the studio by Kevin McCurran, an expert on waste and recycling. So, Kevin, twenty-five million tonnes, that's an awful lot! Where does it all go?

Kevin: Well, Judy the sad truth is that most of it goes underground. In the UK 83% of our waste ends up in landfill sites.

Judy: Really?

Kevin: Yes and these have their own problems. Badly maintained landfills can produce methane gas which then is released into the atmosphere. Methane is known as one of the so-called 'greenhouse gases' which are contributing to global warming.

Judy: So it's not just a space issue? Landfills are also bad for the environment?

Kevin: Absolutely! They can also produce liquids which seep down into the earth and end up polluting our water. Not nice when you consider that landfills contain a vast number of disposable nappies!

Judy: No, indeed not! So, Kevin, it sounds like recycling is the answer.

Kevin: Well, not really. It can help, but a lot of things we use are not recyclable. The best thing we can do to start with is to try and not create so much waste in the first place. We should start re-using things rather than throwing them away.

Judy: So, you mean like taking your plastic bags back to the supermarket and using them again?

Kevin: That's a good place to start.

Judy: And we should start using reusable nappies on our babies?

Kevin: That is a tricky one. Reusable nappies need washing and the kind of detergents we use are not really good for the environment either!

Judy: Oh dear! So, you said 83% of our rubbish goes into the landfills? What about the rest?

Kevin: About nine percent of it is burnt which again makes all sorts of toxins and gases which can harm the atmosphere ...

Judy: And the rest is recycled?

Kevin: Exactly.

Judy: But somebody told me that recycling uses huge amounts of energy which is surely bad in itself?

Kevin: It does consume energy but not as much as not recycling. To recycle a tin can uses five percent of the energy needed to make a new one.

Judy: Well, thanks Kevin for all that information, and I think the message to all of us if re-use if you can and if not, recycle.

Audio scripts

Unit 3

Page 34 Exercise B

Mike: ... thanks very much, Steve. Sounds like we're in for some bad weather again. But now, with some breaking news we're going live to Frank Adie, downtown. Are you there Frank?

Frank: Yes, good afternoon, Mike. I'm here at the Packwell Building where, twenty minutes ago, the death of the media mogul John Packwell was announced. In a statement read by Peter Muller, senior Vice-President of the Packwell Corporation, the tycoon's death took place two hours ago at the City Hospital. Cause of death has not yet been announced, and there were no members of his family present.

Mike: No family? So it was sudden, I guess?

Frank: Apparently Packwell complained of feeling unwell this morning but nobody took that very seriously. He was known as a bit of a hypochondriac. He was admitted to the City Hospital at 12:30, and died there half an hour later.

Mike: This is going to have major repercussions worldwide, isn't it, Frank? I don't think I'm exaggerating when I say that Packwell had media interests on every single continent.

Frank: Actually, Mike, you are.

Mike: I am what?

Frank: You are exaggerating. Penguins don't read newspapers.

Mike: Thank you for that, Frank. So, with the exception of Antarctica, The Packwell Corporation had media interests on every continent. Once again, this is going to have major repercussions worldwide, isn't it, Frank?

Frank: It certainly is. The Corporation has control of 240 newspaper titles, two film production companies, 314 magazine titles, the recently launched web browser, Sherlock, and 300 radio stations including the one you're listening to at this very moment, KCLT Talk Radio. The editorial direction of all these interests is going to give rise to much speculation.

Mike: Could you elaborate a little, Frank?

Frank: Well, the Packwell Corporation has always taken an active interest in the political map of the countries in which it operates, and has always tended to support political candidates from the right. This support has not just been in editorial comment, but in campaign donations as well.

Mike: How about a successor? I realise it's very soon after the event, but Peter Muller, the guy who announced the death, is nearing retirement age. Do you think they'll go for a younger man? Or woman?

Frank: In the ultra-conservative corridors of the Packwell Corporation it is unlikely that a woman will ever take over. None of the senior executives are women. It looked for sometime as though Max Pelet was being groomed for the number one spot, but his standing has suffered since the incident with the chicken. No, Mike; at the moment it's impossible to say who the new boss will be. Likely to be an insider, though.

Mike: Any suggestion of foul play?

Frank: I'm sorry, Mike? Could you repeat that?

Mike: Look, this might sound insensitive, but John Packwell was not one of the world's most popular men. OK, there'll be lots of crocodile tears shed over the next few days, but there are a lot of people who will be sleeping more comfortably tonight knowing that he's gone. So, what do you think? Maybe it wasn't natural causes?

Frank: That is somewhat insensitive! I couldn't possibly speculate on air. There's no suggestion ...

Mike: Come on, Mike! He's gone—life around here will be better without him breathing down our necks! Did he jump or was he pushed?

Frank: Mike, we're on the air.

Mike: You know, Frank? I really don't care anymore. Time to celebrate. That's all from us here at KCLT Talk Radio. We may be back tomorrow.

Page 35 Exercise F

Interviewer: Welcome to Live 2Nite, where we are talking with Wal Cooper, chairman of PBC Communications Network, a multinational that owns about a fifth of America's television and radio and Jennifer Sacks, journalist for the New York Times. Jennifer, at the moment four companies, five companies maybe, control 90 percent of everything we see. Is that a bad idea?

Jennifer: Yes, I think it is. A handful of companies are in charge of everything you get to see through a screen. That's a television screen, not a computer screen. And because all these companies are constantly buying others, you get fewer and fewer people participating in the process of making and delivering news and entertainment. We used to have dozens and dozens of very successful independent production companies producing television programs. Now you have less than a handful.

Interviewer: Wal? What do you think?

Wal: Listen, companies do what companies do. They consolidate, grow bigger, merge and, they get to own the media. I think it's a healthy environment and nobody should really want to change that. Competition is great and it improves the quality of what the public get to see.

Jennifer: Well, I suppose what am I saying is that you can't own every voice there is to own. There should be some limits. And more importantly, what's happened to broadcasting ... broadcasting really used to be ... it used to have a very clear public function. And that's been lost. I really believe you have to keep this in balance. Sure, competition is a good thing, but our Constitution also gives us freedom of speech and the liberty to make up our own mind. If there are too many business interests involved, and let's face it, you big media conglomerates are business for whom the dollar is the bottom line, if there are too many business interests involved, the power comes to lie in the wrong hands.

Interviewer: Wal, where do you go with a good idea these days?

Wal: You know if you've got a great idea, it will come out. It always has been like that. It'll just be owned by one of the large players and, well, really, that's not just an altogether horrible thing, is it? At least you get the opportunity to see your idea come alive.

Jennifer: Yes, that may be the case, but what I do think is these four, five players who believe they are working in an unregulated universe and can determine what people see and hear, should have enough regulation, just enough regulation to stop them from abusing their power. I mean, it has become quite clear that during the Iraq War the American people were not shown everything they should have been shown. Media interests and the government made quite sure of that. I mean it's easy to say ...

Wal: Look, we have more than 500 channels. We have satellite. We have the Internet. I mean these have really changed the media landscape. It's a great diversity, and people can choose what they want to see and hear: every opinion under the sun gets broadcast somewhere. And the idea that the government tells us what to do is mad—we make up our own minds.

Jennifer: But the thing is we don't have more diversity. Instead of it being three channels that were controlled by a few people, there are now 500 channels controlled by a few people. You can't own so much. I mean, the issue here is distribution, it's the ownership of the airwaves, you know. It's the ownership of, so to speak, the broadcast pipes. Or, it's the ownership of the cable pipes. Or it's the ownership of the satellite pipes. That's the issue.

Wal: I agree that distribution is at the centre of it all. But the market will determine where the oil in those pipes goes, Jennifer. You know that. It's a simple ...

Interviewer: Wal, Jennifer, we'll come right back after the break.

Page 41 Exercises B & C

Interviewer: Thank you, Annabel—only you could make bricklaying look such fun. Now, moving on. Today, September 25th is a bit special, though you may not have realised it. It marks the beginning of The American Library Association's Banned Books Week. To tell us a little about it is John Freeman from an organisation called Speak Your Mind. Welcome to the show, John.

John Freeman: Thank you.

Interviewer: Could you tell us a little about the aims of this Banned Books Week, John?

John Freeman: Sure. We're trying to draw people's attention to the issue of censorship. People often think this is an issue of the past; we want to make people understand that it's still very much a current issue.

Interviewer: With all that's bad in the world today – wars, natural disasters – do you think this issue is that important?

John Freeman: Fundamental. Today is the anniversary of the very first Congress of the United States, which took place on September 25th 1789. At that Congress, the first 10 amendments to the Constitution were ratified as the Bill of Rights. The very first amendment guarantees, and I quote, 'Congress shall make no law ... abridging the freedom of speech, or of the press.' In other words, government censorship is unconstitutional.

Interviewer: But the government in the States doesn't ban books, does it?

John Freeman: Not the government as such. It wouldn't dare. But government agencies within the individual states often do?

Interviewer: Really?

John Freeman: An illustrated edition of Little Red Riding Hood was banned in two California school districts in 1989. Why? Because the book shows the heroine taking food and wine to her grandmother. The school districts said they were concerned about the use of alcohol in the story.

Interviewer: All right, that's crazy, but it's an isolated example, right?

John Freeman: You'd like to think so, but nope. Shakespeare's had a rough time recently. In Georgia in 1999 a state-wide newspaper reported that the plays Hamlet, Macbeth and King Lear were being pulled because they might encourage violence. In New Hampshire in 1996 Twelfth

Night suffered a similar fate.

Interviewer: For encouraging violence?

John Freeman: No. Because at one point the heroine disguises herself as a boy. The School Boards were worried that this encouraged what they called 'alternative lifestyles'.

Interviewer: No kidding? But these books weren't actually banned, were they? You could still buy them in the shops?

John Freeman: True, they were banned from schools. Just as in many areas Charles Darwin's Origin of Species is still banned in schools because it contradicts biblical teachings about the creation.

Interviewer: You talk there about 'contradicting biblical teachings', John. Religion seems to be so polarised at the moment; how do religious works fare?

John Freeman: Better than you'd think, actually. Both the Bible and the Koran were banned in the Soviet Union for about 30 years, but are available now. In the modern era, these religious works have tended to be banned for political rather than religious reasons. In one south east Asian country, for example, you can own a copy of the Bible as long as it's not translated into an indigenous language.

Interviewer: Sorry?

John Freeman: You can own a bible as long as you can't understand the language in which it's written.

Interviewer: But we have moved a long way from a time when people or governments burned books?

John Freeman: We have; certainly in parts of the world. But we mustn't get complacent – it's not that long since a European government last burned books.

Interviewer: With the advent of the Internet, do books still have the power that they once did? You can't burn the Internet after all?

John Freeman: You can't burn it, but you can certainly restrict access to it. Books, though, are vital, and have a great symbolic value. The burning of books and, by extension, their banning, tells us that there is something wrong with the society in which it happens. Censorship means that a government doesn't trust its own people. In a democracy we believe that a government works for its people, not against them. But, as we can see, some of the world's greatest democracies need to be reminded of this from time to time.

Interviewer: So, censorship isn't just an issue in the more totalitarian countries?

John Freeman: No, certainly not.

Interviewer: OK, well thank you John. Plenty to think about there. Thanks for joining us today.

John Freeman: You're welcome.

Interviewer: Now, it's time for our regular cookery feature with Tabitha Bush.

Page 42 Exercise E

1   The play had been running for a month during the authorities pulled it.
2   Many people walked out since the performance.
3   Positions became polarised after an argument at the two leaders.
4   The best news is in the BBC.
5   The government banned the book through complaints from the public.

Audio scripts

Unit 4

Page 50 Exercises B & C & Page 51 Exercise D

Roger Day: The latest figures from a Royal College of Physicians survey, suggests that many hospitals in the UK are failing their heart attack patients. This is quite alarming since heart disease is the biggest killer in the UK today, exacerbated by poor diet and smoking. In the studio, we have Dr Jane Moore, a leading myocardial expert who is going to talk us through the report. So, Dr Moore, what exactly is this report all about?

Jane Moore: Well, Roger, as you said heart disease is the biggest killer in the UK today, and also the most expensive drain on our health services today. In order to ascertain whether hospitals were allocating their resources efficiently in this area, the Royal College of Physicians set two targets, just over a year ago, to measure hospital performance against. On the surface of it, the report is quite alarming as fewer than 20% of hospitals managed to achieve both targets. When you look at the results in more detail, things are not quite as bad as that figure makes it seem.

Roger Day: Fewer than 20% sounds terrible though, and I am sure there are going to be lots of potential heart patients out there who will be quite worried by this.

Jane Moore: This is true, but really there is no cause for alarm. Let's look at what the targets were. Firstly, when a heart attack victim presents in the Accident and Emergency department, they receive a shot of anti-blood clotting drugs. The first target was to ensure that patients receive this shot within 30 minutes of the heart attack. The figures show that about 30% of hospitals achieved this target.

Roger Day: That's not good.

Jane Moore: Not on the surface, but typically, many heart attack patients only present in the hospital 20 to 25 minutes after the attack. Many mistake the symptoms for other things and so delay seeking medical help. Once they are in the hospital, there can be delays in the diagnosis, which leads to the shot not being given until more than 30 minutes after the event.

Roger Day: I see. So what was the second target?

Jane Moore: The second target was to ensure that when patients returned home, they continued to take drugs to prevent further heart attacks. These include statins, beta-blockers as well as aspirin.

Roger Day: We have all heard of aspirin but what are the other two?

Jane Moore: Statins are drugs that are used to lower cholesterol. High levels of cholesterol, caused by a fatty diet, is one of the major causes of heart disease today. Beta-blockers are used to treat high blood-pressure, or hypertension, by slowing the heart down. This reduces strain on the organ.

Roger Day: Right, so how many hospitals managed to hit the target?

Jane Moore: Well, just over 50% of departments managed this which is quite a good figure when you realise that people have a choice as to whether they actually take the medicine which is prescribed for them.

Roger Day: Well, absolutely ...

Jane Moore: So, taking these two figures together fewer than 20% of hospitals managed to hit both targets. I think however, that this should be seen as positive news, since this was the first audit that had been done on hosptials' performance in this area, so they just didn't know what their performance was. Now they know, they can develop strategies to improve this.

Roger Day: This is true and I guess we will have to wait another year to find out. Well, that's all we have time for, so thank you Jane for coming in and explaining all that to us.

Page 56 Exercise A

Breast cancer is a major concern for all women. One out of every nine women will develop breast cancer over the next year. While the statistics show that more and more women are surviving breast cancer, it is probable that one in twenty-seven will die from it. As with HIV / AIDS, there is an overt effort to raise funds for breast cancer research and its cure. The most prominent symbol for breast cancer awareness is the little pink ribbon and many groups and organisations hold annual events, such as the CIBC Run for the Cure in Canada, as fundraisers that provide the opportunity for survivors and family members of breast cancer victims to come together and share their stories.

Although all forms of cancer are devastating, breast cancer has come to the foreground over the last few years. It is not just a disease for women either. Men can also contract breast cancer. Even though the statistics for men are much lower than for women, it is becoming more common in males. There is no finite age group targeted for this disease since cancer can occur in anyone at any time. The best prevention is to visit your doctor for annual check-ups and have a breast exam. Women aged fifty and older should also get a mammogram every 2 years that will help to catch any early signs of tumours or lumps in the tissue of the breasts. Many doctors are also teaching their patients how to administer self-examinations so that any irregular formations that may appear in between check-ups can be detected early on.

Researchers and physicians do not know what causes cancer. A healthy lifestyle of a low-fat diet and regular exercise definitely helps reduce the risk of contracting cancer yet even healthy people can be afflicted. Family history also plays a part in so far as a person whose mother or grandmother has had or died from breast cancer are at a higher risk of getting it themselves. This is all the more reason for women to be regularly examined. If a lump is detected, a doctor must determine the status of the lump. Benign lumps are common in older women where the tissue in the breast has hardened but is not cancerous. Malignant tumours are cancerous and surgery is often recommended to remove it before the cancer has the opportunity to spread to other areas of the body followed by rounds of chemotherapy or radiation therapy.

Until a cure is found, education and awareness of breast cancer will continue to be the leading form of prevention. October has now been declared as 'Breast Cancer Awareness' month and many commercial companies, such as the candy M&M's, and retailers promote awareness during this month by selling special products in the famed pink colour, donating a high percentage of their profits to breast cancer research.

Page 60 Exercise C

1   Anorexia and bulimia are the two most common types of eating disorders.

2   In both cases, a person suffers from a distorted body image of themselves.

3   While both mostly affect women, 10% of the male population suffers from the disorder, too.

4   A common error is that people believe the person has lost their appetite.

5   Many anorexic victims see a fat person when they look in the mirror but they are actually losing weight and are terribly under-weight.

6   Bulimia is the opposite of anorexia as people binge on food and then force themselves to get rid of it.

7   Bulimics can look like a normal sized person so it is difficult to detect a person with bulimia just by looking at them.

8   Symptoms of anorexia include denial of hunger, excessive exercising, a dramatic loss in body weight in a short time and withdrawal from social activities.

9   Symptoms of bulimia are eating a lot of food but not gaining any weight, excusing themselves after eating to go to the bathroom, not participating in social activities and using laxatives.

10 Both disorders tend to occur in the teenage years, between the ages of 14–18, and can be life threatening if not detected and treated.

Page 66 Exercises B & C

HP: Hello and welcome to today's edition of *The World Around Us*; I'm Hank Philips. Now, over the last few years, people's appetite for dangerous activities seems to have been on the increase. You only have to browse the shelves of your local store to see the large number of magazines devoted to extreme sports. Also, although health professionals have helped us to see the dangers inherent in pursuits that we once thought harmless, such as smoking and drinking liquor, people still continue to do them. So, what is it about this risk-taking behaviour that makes it so attractive to people? Our guest in the studio is Professor Robert Wilson, an expert in the psychology of risks, who is going to help us find out. So, Professor Wilson, why do people want to behave in such a way?

PW: Well, Hank, in order to understand why people take risks we first need to look at what risk is. Risk, can be defined as the probability that some undesirable event will happen, usually as the result of our behaviour. When deciding whether to take a risk or not, we balance what we perceive that probability to be against whatever we feel we can gain from the activity. For example, people who smoke knowing the health risks, will weigh up what they perceive the likelihood of their contracting a smoking related disease is, against the pleasure that they obtain from the nicotine.

HP: I see. But don't we make decisions like that all the time? For example, I'm terrified of flying, but am willing to take the risk as I enjoy being in foreign countries and know that the statistical likelihood of that plane going down is very small...

PW: Exactly, that is a perfect example of the way risks present themselves as everyday challenges. In fact, we believe that we have evolved as a species to take risks in order to survive. Primitive man would weigh up the likelihood of a wild animal wounding or killing him against the gain of having food for his family.

HP: Right, so what you are saying is that risk taking behaviour is part of what has made humans such a successful species?

PW: You've got it Hank.

HP: But if that is true, why do people exhibit different levels of willingness to take risks? My eldest son, for example is really into extreme sports but his younger brother thinks he's crazy and prefers much less risky hobbies.

PW: Well, the current view is that people fall into three categories: risk avoiders, risk reducers and risk optimisers. Risk avoiders, will stay away from what we would consider risky behaviour, they are the ones who play it safe.

HP: Sure sounds like Chuck ...

PW: Risk reducers are people who will perform risky actions even though they are aware of the risks because they feel that the gain outweighs the risk. These people will have a limit where they think that the risks outweigh the gains. Now, risk optimisers are people who will engage in risk taking activity because of the risk involved, that is what attracts them and often the riskier the better.

HP: And that sounds like Hank junior. So what makes people fall into each category? Is it something that occurs in childhood or...

PW: Well, we currently think that it is part of what makes up your personality. Recent evidence also suggest that it could be genetic, some of us have risky genes.

HP: That is interesting as I don't like taking risks too much whereas my wife will try anything once. So I guess Hank junior takes after his mother and Chuck takes after me ... literally ...

PW: That's right.

HP: But that doesn't explain why different people are prepared to take different kinds of risk. For example, many businessmen risk their shirts on the stock market every day, but they don't all go bungee jumping at the weekend...

PW: Well, recent studies have divided risk taking into the following four categories. The first is referred to as 'thrill seeking'. This trait is associated with taking physical risks, like Hank junior. A second category is 'experience seeking', gaining new experiences from risks and this is associated with all kinds of behaviour. The third category is 'lack of inhibition'. This is associated with what could be called social risks, such as drinking, smoking or drug taking. The final category is the 'boredom threshold'. Some people get bored more easily and will take risks to combat this.

HP: I see. Well, like all things connected to the human mind it sounds quite complicated but thank you Professor Wilson for leading us through these issues in such an easy to follow manner. And if any of you would like to know more, *Why Take Risks?* by Professor Robert Wilson is available in all good bookstores. Next week we will be taking a look at... (fade)

Susie: Hi Brian! So how was Australia? I hope you've brought me back lots of photos, you know how I like photos!

Brian: Well, I only took a few ... hundred that is! It was absolutely amazing, so much to do and the scenery was stunning. I've brought my laptop round as I only took a digital camera.

Susie: Great, set it up on the table and I'll make some coffee. White one sugar, right?

Brian: You remembered ...

(a few minutes pass)

Susie: So, there you go, white one sugar. Now, let's see these photos.

Brian: Right, so this is me in front of the Sydney Opera House, this is me in front of Sydney Harbour Bridge ...

Susie: I recognise it... it looks bigger than I imagined ...

Brian: It is quite big ... now this next one is the view from the top of the Harbour Bridge ...

Susie: That looks terrifying! You know me I hate heights ...

Brian: Wait till you see the ones of the bungee jumping then ...

Susie: You went bungee jumping?!

Brian: Yep! That was when I was at Surfer's Paradise. Well, you know me, I'm a born risk taker, I saw a sign saying bungee jumping and just had to do it.

Susie: Rather you than me!

Brian: Look here we go ... this is me on top of the bridge about to go ... and ... there! Whew, I can still feel the adrenaline rush ...

Susie: But it looks so dangerous!

Brian: Well, of course there are risks, but the leaflet from the bungee jumping centre said that statistically it is about as dangerous as driving one hundred miles in a car, that's like from here to London. There have been literally millions of jumps and you can count the accidents on the fingers of one hand ... well two hands I think...

Susie: I would just be thinking that I was about to be one of those fingers!

Brian: And as long as you go to a reputable centre then you will be fine. The one I was at seemed very safety conscious ...

Susie: One thing I have always wanted to know is, how do you get back on the bridge after jumping?

Brian: In some places they let a rope down and hoist you up again. I think that would be really scary. Here the jump was over water, so they lowered me down on the bungee and somebody came round in a boat and picked me up. Look, here is one of me getting into the boat...

Susie: Oh yes. Look at your face! You look terrified!

Brian: Well, I suppose I was! When I was up on the bridge, I almost chickened out, but the staff were very good and made me feel very supported. I could hear my heart beating in my head ... it was quite unnerving! Then they did a count down from five to one and then I just leant forward and went. It was only a few seconds but it seemed to take an age. I was also convinced that I was going to hit the water...

Susie: I always imagine it is going to be like the sensation when you go over a hill in a car and your stomach feels as if it is in your mouth ... only worse ...

Brian: Well, yes, it is a bit like that.

Susie: I bet it hurt when the bungee got to its full length and stopped you ...

Brian: Actually, that part was surprisingly gentle! I must say, I had been worried about that, but the harnesses they use are so good ...

Susie: So what is the actual bungee made of?

Brian: Well, they used to use rubber cords sheathed in cotton, but we were using the latest type of all-rubber cord. Apparently, it is made of about a thousand small strands all joined together... and it stretches to four times its length when you jump so it is surprisingly short ...

Susie: I don't know ... trust those Australians to come up with something like that ...

Brian: Actually, they told us at the centre that it is based on something that the natives of a group of South Pacific islands do. They use vines instead of rubber, and apparently the first modern bungee jump was off the Clifton suspension bridge in Bristol in 1978, so it was us Brits that started it!

Susie: Mmm ..., well you wouldn't catch me doing it. So, would you do it again?

Brian: Well, I did actually! I jumped five times in total, twice backwards ... now that was scary!

Page 85 Exercises D & E

P: Good morning and welcome to *Education Matters*, the magazine programme for parents and teachers. Now, last week a mother from Gloucestershire was sent to prison for the second time in a year, for allowing her children to play truant. The law was changed last November to allow custodial sentences for parents who fail to combat their children's truancy. To discuss this I have with me in the studio John Rawlings, junior Education Minister and Graham Howarth from the pressure group Campaign for Penal Reform. Now, Minister, if I could turn to you first. This woman spent 28 days of a three month sentence in prison earlier on this year, and last week she was sentenced to a further 28 days. Isn't this evidence that your new law just isn't working?

JR: No, not at all. On the contrary, statistics which were released by the Association of Schoolmasters yesterday, show that since the new law was introduced, the instance of truancy across the country has fallen by 30%.

P: But this mother hasn't seemed to learn her lesson.

JR: Although I don't want to get drawn into a discussion on this particular case, following the mother's first imprisonment her daughter's attendance at school did actually increase to acceptable levels, and remained so for some months. It was only in the last few weeks that her attendance dropped off dramatically.

P: If I could bring Graham Howarth in for a moment. Graham, your pressure groups opposed this law from the outset didn't you?

GH: Absolutely. We believe that this law allowing parents to be imprisoned is not only cruel, but can actually be detrimental to children's home life. Although we agree that a good education can be a very valuable asset, this law seeks to protect that at the cost of taking a parent out of the family home for a period of up to three months. They're therefore unable to supervise and discipline their children at home during this period. And what about the case of a single parent? That could result in further upheaval, as children would have to be taken into care.

JR: The courts have full sentencing guidelines which they use to avoid the kind of hardship which you have just described, but let's look at the figures. As I have already said, truancy has fallen by 30% since this law was introduced. Fewer than ten parents have actually been jailed under the new law, out of the 7,500 parents who are prosecuted for not ensuring their children attend school every year.

GH: Well, it's ten too many for me. But what about parents who do everything in their power to try and get their children to go to school but can't. I have seen case studies which include a mother of a 15-year-old boy who locks himself in his bedroom, and refuses to leave point blank. At 15 he is physically a man, and there is nothing his mother can do to compel him.

JR: And the law would protect her in that case. Let us be clear here, the law does not allow any parent who fails to ensure that their child goes to school to be jailed. It has to be proven that the parent actually condones their child's behaviour. It is all about setting a good example.

GH: Does setting a good example mean administering an extremely draconian penalty for what is a victimless offence? What happened to the principle of the punishment fitting the crime?

JR: I do not call depriving a child of a decent education a victimless crime. The child is every bit a victim of the parent's negligence in this.

P: OK, so, Graham. Your organisation would repeal this law, which notwithstanding its slightly draconian appearance, does seem to be working. How would you like to see the Government combating truancy?

GH: Statistics show that poverty and failing schools tend to go hand in hand with truancy. Parents who have to work two jobs in order to provide a roof over their children's heads are often not at home in the morning to ensure that their children go to school. Schools which are providing substandard education are failing to inspire their pupils who do not attend school, as they are bored. Also, truancy has been linked to some kinds of attention deficit disorder which has recently been linked to poor diet and malnutrition. Our solution is to combat poverty and to raise school standards, and this will in turn cut truancy.

JR: Well, our Government is working to make improvements in both of these areas, but statistics show that our new law is working.

P: John Rawlings, Graham Howarth, thank you very much. Well, next week on *Education Matters*, we will be looking at...

TS: The recent news that in England a 16-year-old child has just been awarded a degree from the prestigious Oxford University has been wowing people on both sides of the Atlantic. Sufiah Yusof is not the youngest person to have been awarded a degree from that institution. That honour belongs to Ruth Lawrence who graduated in 1985 aged just 15. Like Yusof, Lawrence had been taught by her parents at home, instead of opting for state schooling, and home schooling is a growing trend here in the States as well as in Europe. Although, home school students do not always make the same lofty achievements as Yusof and Lawrence, nevertheless home-school students do seem to make faster progress than those attending regular school. In the studio today we have Jeanette Graupinski from Denver, Colorado, who has come in to tell us about her experiences home schooling her 14-year-old son, Marcus. So Jeanette, welcome to the show.

JG: Thank you very much, and may I say it's a pleasure to be here today, Todd.

TS: So Jeanette, what was it that first decided you to teach your son at home.

JG: Well Todd, there were a great many factors involved. Firstly, when I started home schooling Marcus two years ago, there had been two teacher strikes in the previous 12 months, and we were getting to a situation where, in my opinion, the local School Board and the teachers were playing the students off against each other like pawns. But I had been unhappy with the school Marcus was at for a while. I felt the students were not getting a good enough moral lead from the staff, class sizes seemed to grow and grow every year, it was just a mess. It was also coming up to the time that Marcus would be starting High School, and looking round at the local public schools I was not impressed. The one public school that I thought might be right for Marcus involved a trip of almost an hour on the school bus, and we just couldn't afford to send him to a private school. Then one day, I got talking to a girlfriend of mine who had been home schooling her daughter for a couple of years and raved about it.

TS: So, you took your child out of school and started teaching him yourself?

JG: That's right. We had to get permission of from the local School Board, which involved a home visit, when they interviewed Marcus and myself, but then we were able to start almost immediately.

TS: So what benefits do you think Marcus has gained from the new arrangements?

JG: Well, the first thing I noticed was how confident he became with our adult friends. Spending most of his time with his parents, rather than other children, made him mature quite quickly. I also noticed how polite he was compared to the neighbour's kids, but

that's another story. Also, he has progressed quite quickly with his lessons. As we can choose to spend a little more time on the subjects that he likes, he has advanced more quickly in those areas, and we are currently studying things that he wouldn't have done until his senior year, in mathematics and geography.

TS: Wow, that's like a whole two-year head start!

JG: Exactly.

TS: Don't you think there's a chance that Marcus is maybe suffering from not having schoolmates of his own age?

JG: That worried me a lot. My girlfriend had advised us to find some local clubs for him to take part in, to allow him to mix with kids of his own age, and so he goes to the local swimming club twice a week. He also played Little League Football, but he has gotten a bit big for that now.

TS: Right. So if somebody came to you today and asked for your top five pieces of advice for home schooling their kid, what would you say?

JG: Well, firstly, I would point out that home schooling is very intensive for the parent. I am with Marcus 24 / 7 and rarely have any time on my own. That can be a big strain which I am not sure everybody could take.

TS: Yes, I hadn't thought of that. One things of the effect it will have on the child but one seldom considers the effects on the parents.

JG: That's right, so it's something people should be aware of, Secondly, it can be quite a financial strain. There are extra books and materials that you need to buy but also the parent who is acting as teacher cannot work outside the home, so you need to be sure that you can afford it. Luckily, I was a housewife before I started home schooling Marcus, but I have known people who have given up work to teach their kids. Thirdly, having people around the house all day sure messes it up! I was amazed at how much more cleaning I was having to do! Also, don't worry if you don't feel confident enough to teach your kids. I often find myself learning along with Marcus. As long as you can read and write you can help your kids find their way around the materials. This also helps your children to become more independent learners, which will benefit them greatly in the long run. Finally, be sure that your child is up for home schooling. Many parents force it on their kids who don't really want it and that can create a lot of tension. We sat down with Marcus and discussed it and in fact he had been bullied a little at Junior High, and so was quite happy to be taught in a home school environment.

TS: Well, I must say Jeanette that it sounds like it's working for you, and if you at home want more information about any of the issues in today's programme, contact us on 303-767-8000, that's 303-767-8000. So, thank you Jeanette for sharing your advice with us today and tune in next week for more *Family Values*.

Audio scripts

Unit 7

Page 98 Exercise C

Speaker 1

Ann: Excuse me, sir; do you speak any foreign languages?

Man: Why you wanna know?

Ann: It's for my college course. Do you speak any?

Man: Merican's always been good enough for me. Don't have time to waste on no foreign stuff.

Ann: Thank you.

Speaker 2

Ann: Excuse me, madam; do you speak any foreign languages?

Woman: No, I don't. I'd love to though.

Ann: Why don't you learn?

Woman: Full-time job, three young children? Why do you think?

Ann: OK. Thanks very much.

Speaker 3

Ann: Sir? Sir? Could I ask you a question?

Man: Oh dear; if you really must.

Ann: Do you speak any foreign languages?

Man: Why on earth would I want to do that? I speak the language of Shakespeare, the language of Wordsworth. I speak the language of an empire that once ruled most of the world. I don't do 'foreign'.

Ann: Oh. Right. Um, thank you.

Speaker 4

Ann: Excuse me, madam; do you speak any foreign languages?

Woman: Yes, I do—one.

Ann: Excellent. What do you speak?

Woman: English.

Ann: No, sorry; do you speak any foreign language?

Woman: English is a foreign language to me. I'm Swedish.

Ann: I'm sorry. Your English is excellent. Would you say you were fluent?

Woman: I'd like to be! I really don't know. It seems hard to judge exactly what fluency is. I certainly need it to survive here.

Ann: Thank you so much.

Speaker 5

Ann: Excuse me; do you speak any foreign languages?

Man: I try. I'm learning Indonesian. I've been at it for 20 years.

Ann: Why Indonesian?

Man: Indonesian women! The most beautiful in the world!

Ann: Are you fluent yet?

Man: About as fluent as the average 2-year-old. Never seem to get beyond mau makan sama saya?

Ann: What does that mean?

Man: Would you like to have dinner with me?

Speaker 6

Ann: Excuse me; do you speak any foreign languages?

Woman: Yes. Spanish, Italian. I love the Romance languages.

Ann: So, you're looking for a boyfriend?

Woman: I beg your pardon?

Ann: Oh. Um, sorry. Would you say you were fluent in both?

Woman: My Italian's better than my Spanish. That's pretty good I think. As long as I can get by, that's enough for me. I was posted to Rome by my company for a few years. Best way to get a language under your belt, I think.

Page 99 Exercise E

Lecturer: Right. Are there any more questions before we go home? Yes; the gentleman in the blue sweater.

Man: Thanks. How do people who make dictionaries actually come up with the definitions for the words? How does someone really know what a word means? Our teacher asked us to come up with a definition for fluency - it was tricky!

Lecturer: Good question. What does a word actually mean? Do you have a good dictionary?

Man: Yeah; it's ok, I think.

Lecturer: Does it include etymologies?

Man: Um ... what are they?

Lecturer: The best dictionaries will include the etymology of a word. The etymology tells us where the word comes from. If you're using a bilingual dictionary then it's unlikely to have them. Let's take your word as an example. 'Fluency.' OK. The first recorded use of the word was 1599, over 400 years ago. The word comes from the Latin verb fluere which means to flow. That gives us a good clue - and the earliest use of the word meant to move like water, easily and smoothly. A dancer's movements might be described as fluent using the word with this meaning.

Man: But that's not really the meaning we're looking for, is it?

Lecturer: No, but you can see how it's related, I'm sure. Later, the word was used to describe someone's ability with language. So, fluency became the ability to speak with ease, smoothly or without hesitation. It's speech that flows.

Man: Awesome. And that comes from that Latin word?

Lecturer: It certainly does, and so do other things. The Latin word that gives us an English word for flowing speech also gives us the English word 'flush', throwing water down the toilet. Perhaps someone a long time ago was making a joke - many words spoken easily are no better than what we throw down the toilet! Isn't the English language a wonderful thing?!!

Page 104 Exercises C & D and Page 105 Exercises E & F

Welcome to the Dyslexia Information Service. Here you can hear all about dyslexia and what to do when you think you or somebody close to you has this condition.

Press 1 to continue.

Many children experience some difficulties learning to read, write, and spell. With access to appropriate teaching most of these children can and do become good readers. However, if after receiving high-quality instruction, a child fails to develop fluent reading abilities, he or she may be identified as dyslexic. A child identified as dyslexic can learn to read, but their reading often remains slower than their peers', and the effort required for reading remains substantially greater. Nonetheless, many dyslexics not only graduate from High School and college but go on to excel in a wide variety of occupations.

Dyslexia is the inability to learn to read fluently, despite otherwise normal intellectual functions, but no single definition of dyslexia is accepted by all reading specialists. However, a central feature of all definitions is an unexpected and substantial difficulty in learning to read. Other symptoms include a tendency to write words and letters in reversed sequences, similar reversals of words and letters in the person's speech, and illegible handwriting. The lack of a commonly accepted definition of dyslexia has caused some teachers, doctors, and researchers to avoid using the term altogether.

Press 2 to continue.

Because there is no clear and widely held definition of the problem, estimates of the number of people with dyslexia vary widely. Most researchers have suggested that dyslexia is rare, occurring in 1 to 2 per cent of the world's population. However, others believe that 10 to 20 per cent of the population has dyslexia or display dyslexic characteristics. Those arguing for the higher incidence levels also suggest that dyslexia can appear in differing levels of intensity, affecting the reading achievement of some individuals more than others. Dyslexia is usually identified during childhood, and continues to affect individuals throughout their lives, though only a few dyslexics remain non-readers into adulthood.

Evidence suggests that dyslexia is more common in some families than others. Because of this, some researchers claim that there may be a genetic basis for dyslexia, but this has not been conclusively proved. Most studies have also reported that dyslexia affects significantly more boys than girls. However, a recent large-scale study reported that although schools identified more boys with reading problems than girls, test results showed severe reading difficulties in roughly equivalent numbers of both sexes.

Press 3 to continue.

Common methods of diagnosing dyslexia vary widely, although most experts rule out other common sources of learning difficulty — such as lack of intelligence, absence from school, hearing or vision problems, and behaviour disorders—before making a diagnosis of dyslexia. Many researchers have called for a shift in methods to identify dyslexia. Some argue that a diagnosis of dyslexia should be made only in children who continue to struggle with reading, even after having received high-quality, intensive tutorial instruction. This diagnostic method consists of two steps. First, experts assess the intensity and appropriateness of the instruction the child has received. If they find no evidence of an appropriate, intensive educational intervention to correct reading problems, then a diagnosis of dyslexia is premature. Second, experts assess the child's ability to distinguish phonemes, the individual sounds that make up words. Once again, a diagnosis of dyslexia would be premature if examiners identified difficulties in this area, but found that the child had received no intervention to develop phonological processing skills.

Experts diagnose dyslexia only when reliable evidence shows that a child's reading difficulties do not seem correctable through intensive, appropriate instruction. A child may not respond well in group instructional settings and may fall behind classmates in both reading acquisition and phonological processing skills. But these deficits alone would not warrant a diagnosis of dyslexia. Such a diagnosis is appropriate only if the deficits remain after the child receives intensive tutorial instruction to correct them. Thank you for calling the Dyslexia Information Service. Replace your handset, or press 1 to return to the start of the message.

Page 114 Exercise C

Dr Jones: Good morning, ladies and gentlemen and welcome to the first lecture of the new semester. I'm Doctor Jones. This course - The History of Language - will be run by me and Doctor Wilson. Unlike my colleague, I am prepared to accept interruptions during my talk as long as they are short and to the point. There will, of course, be the usual question and answer session at the end. OK, who can tell me, what is a dictionary?

Student 1: A book that tells you what words mean?

Dr Jones: A book? Does it have to be a book?

Student 2: I guess not, but it usually is. It's a list of words arranged in alphabetical order which tells you their meanings.

Dr Jones: Just their meanings? OK. A dictionary is, indeed, a listing of words, usually in alphabetical order, with their meanings or equivalents.

Student 3: Their equivalents?

Dr Jones: Yes. Think of a bilingual dictionary. They just give you a translation. The equivalent of a word in another language. Now, dictionaries can also give you other information like pronunciations, syllabications to help you with the word stress, etymologies, that's the history of the word, and examples of the word's usage.

The earliest known dictionaries were kept in the Mesopotamian city of Elba which is now part of modern day Syria. They were clay tablets inscribed in about the 2300 BC and consist of words in the Sumerian language and their equivalents in the Akkadian language. Other early dictionaries, mostly written after the 5th century AD, include lists of Sanskrit, Tibetan, Mongolian, and Chinese and translations into other languages. Perhaps the most outstanding achievement of this early period was that of the Arab scholar Khalil ibn Ahmad who, in the 8th century or thereabouts, compiled a dictionary of the entire Arabic vocabulary. Yes?

Student 3: I'm surprised that we've reached the 8th century without any mention of the Greeks or the Romans.

Dr Jones: That is a very good point. Neither the Greeks nor the Romans were great lexicographers. It was the first century AD before either produced any work of note. We will be returning to this in a week or so. Thanks.

OK. The earliest multilingual dictionary of what we might call modern times appeared in 1502 and was the work of an Italian monk called Ambrogio Calepino. It was written in Latin and included equivalents in Greek, Italian, French and Spanish. When it was revised in 1590 this was taken up to eleven languages. Among the first major dictionaries to be written entirely in modern languages, rather than in Latin, were written in Italian, Spanish and French.

Student 1: Not in English?

Dr Jones: Most certainly not. We're about to come to English dictionaries but it might be worth stopping for a moment. English as a world language is a modern phenomenon. Always bear that in mind. At this time, the 16th century, far more people spoke Italian, French or Spanish than spoke English. It's true that the English language was about to enter a remarkable period, but at this time it was a language spoken by a relatively small number of people on an island off the coast of north-west Europe.

But we can't ignore it, can we? In 1440 in Norfolk, a part of England, a monk called Galfridus Grammaticus compiled a list of 10,000 English words, with their Latin equivalents. It was printed in 1499 by someone with the splendid name of Wynkyn de Worde and has a good claim to be the first English dictionary. In 1604, Robert Cawdrey produced the first dictionary giving definitions of English words in English; and in 1623 the word dictionary was used for the first time by Henry Cockeram in *The English Dictionarie*. These early works characteristically confined themselves to 'hard words' and phrases not generally understood, because the daily vocabulary of the language was not expected to require definitions. The *New English Dictionary* of 1702 by John Kersey departed from this tradition by including ordinary English words as well as unfamiliar terms. Another early work of note was the *Universal Etymological English Dictionary*, published in 1721 by Nathan Bailey. This work used quotations from literary works to confirm definitions. Then, in 1755, *A Dictionary of the English Language*, by essayist and literary critic Samuel Johnson, further extended the use of quotations. Johnson's two-volume dictionary remained the model of English lexicography for more than a century until the appearance of, perhaps, the most famous dictionary of all time. Does anyone know the dictionary I mean?

Scholars more and more felt the need for a full historical dictionary that would display the English language in accordance with scientific principles of lexicography. The Philological Society, founded in 1842, devised plans for, what was to be called, *A New English Dictionary on Historical Principles*. Work began, but it wasn't until the appointment of the brilliant James Murray in 1879 that work advanced speedily. Part one was finished in 1884, but so painstaking was the work that it wasn't finished until 1928 in over 15,500 pages. It was reprinted in 1933 in 12 volumes under the title *The Oxford English Dictionary*, and *as the OED* it has been known ever since. A second edition wasn't ready until 1989, and was published in 20 volumes. It was, and remains, an outstanding achievement.

The first important contribution to lexicography in the United States was *The American Spelling Book*, issued in 1783 by educator and lexicographer Noah Webster. Although not a true dictionary, *The American Spelling Book*, because of its American origin and emphasis and its simplification of English, became a household reference wordbook throughout the United States. Its success led Webster to compile *A Compendious Dictionary of the English Language* in 1806. He then embarked upon his major contribution to lexicography, *An American Dictionary of the English Language*, begun in 1807 and published in 1828. This ambitious work included 12,000 more words and 40,000 more definitions than any previous dictionary of the English language. But despite its emphasis on typically American usage, distinguished from British usage, this work was never popular. Webster was largely responsible for the simplification of spelling in what is now known as American English.

Right, I'm afraid that's all we've got time for today. It's a huge topic as you can see. At our next meeting we'll discuss further advances in American lexicography and how modern techniques are affecting the way dictionaries are compiled. Any questions before we head home?

Page 115 Exercise E

1

a: South.

b: North.

a: No, it's on the south coast. Look it up if you don't believe me.

2

c: Look at that. Isn't it just adorable?

d: Do you think it's a bit expensive?

c: Expensive? It's your daughter's wedding for heaven's sakes. Just imagine how you'd look in that. No one would even look at the groom's mother. Worth every penny!

3

e: It's 'ie' not 'ei', Steve.

f: Well, my spell checker isn't complaining.

e: Steve ... it's 'ie' not 'ei'.

f: OK, cleverdick. But I'm going to look it up first.

4

g: Do you remember that film *Four Weddings And A Funeral*? What was the poem that the guy read out at the funeral?

h: I can't remember the title, but it was by WH Auden. Why?

g: Nothing important. I just like it.

h: Well it's a famous poem. Try and find it in here, I know it has lots of modern poetry.

5

i: Ah, look at that. Wasn't he beautiful?

j: He was. And do you remember when you took it? I said he's not going to thank you when he's 30 showing things like this to his friends.

i: Oh yeah. Mind you, Ethel, he was 2 when we took it.

j: Yeah. Beautiful all the same.

6

k: I always use the online version. Saves having loads of books lying around the house.

l: Is it any good?

k: Brilliant. Look, you just type a word in here, and it searches for all the articles with that word. The most likely one is at the top of the list.

l: Expensive?

k: Cheaper than 25 volumes; and you get free annual updates online.

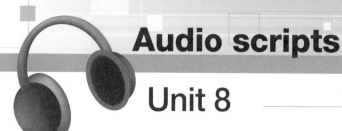

Page 120 Exercise B

T: Come in and sit down. Rosa, first I would like to explain to you that this meeting is more for your benefit than anything else.

R: What do you mean?

T: Well, the best research paper this year will receive not only a grade of excellence but will also allow the writer to choose from three writing scholarships to Yale, Columbia or Harvard Universities.

R: Really! Oh my God. I had no idea. I would have done a better job had I known.

T: Rosa your work is beyond excellent and as a member of the board of judges it is our duty to check your work in detail. Ok? can we begin then?

R: Yes, Mr Kennedy.

T: Tell us first of all how did you come up with the topic?

R: Well as you know, my family and I came to the United States when I was seven. Not being able to speak the language, I was placed in what they called back then the Pilot Bilingual Program. Basically that meant that I was assigned a tutor to explain anything I did not understand in class. I can't tell you how much of a help that was, not only for me, but also for my teachers and my parents. This is how I came up with the topic. Today more than 20 years later, there are still kids who like me need the help of those tutors in order to make it in school.

T: Oh, so you would say that a lot of personal input went into your work.

R: Oh yes! But just a little. Our teacher told us where to find all sorts of information. I used encyclopaedias, atlases thesauri, dictionaries, web directories, etc. I had to cross reference again and again to finally find what I was looking for. At times it took me 20 steps before reaching the right source. Since I wanted it to be easy to read I used a thesaurus to find other ways of saying words that in my opinion were a bit complicated.

T: What did you use to check your grammar?

R: Well the dictionary helped me a lot. In it I found verb forms, adjective forms and I used it to make sure I was using the right words. Oh and a grammar handbook too.

T: What use did you give to the encyclopaedia.

R: Well as you can see, I wrote my research paper with some background information full of facts about the history of bilingual education and throughout the paper I gave my readers data that would support what I was saying.

T: Did you write the source of the information in your bibliography?

R: Oh yes! but a lot of the times I paraphrased my findings in my own words so this way it was my own work. Well that's what Mrs Jones recommended.

T: What other reference books did you use?

R: I used almanacs to find out about population percentages per state. I used a gazetteer to locate geographical information. When I wrote about the pioneers of bilingual education I had to use a biographical index to find more about them. But I'd say between the encyclopaedia and the Internet search engines, these helped me the most. With the actual writing I'd say the thesaurus and a good english grammar handbook were what I used the most.

T: OK sounds like you followed all the necessary guidelines. How much of what you wrote came from research using reference books?

R : I'd say most of it but using my own words made it more my work.